THE ULTIMATE

HANDBOOK FOR

PARENTING TEENAGERS

7 Important Conversations You Must Have For

Connecting, Supporting, Mentoring, and Empowering

Your Teens For Success Through High School and Life

KATHY WYNNE

TABLE OF CONTENTS

A Free Gift To Our Readers

20 Proven Strategies To Stop Homework
Procrastination can be ready to use right away!
Visit this link:

www.allforparentingteens.com

INTRODUCTION

- ➲ Do you worry about how it will be for your teen's future?
- ➲ Are you afraid that you are not providing enough parental supervision?
- ➲ Do you have communication issues with your teen?

Being a parent is one of the most significant stages in your life. It is rewarding to witness your child accomplish every milestone. Nevertheless, it can also be one of the most difficult when you worry about your ability to guide and support your child. This is certainly true when your child becomes a teenager.

Many parents of teens face challenges, and your affirmative answers to the above questions are just some of the many pains that parents are going through when their kids reach the stage of adolescence. During

1

such crucial times, you worry that your teens may drop out of school, get pregnant, experiment with sex, get into drugs and alcohol, break the rules, have too much exposure to social media, and jeopardize their future careers.

According to Cleveland Clinic, from the age of 13 to 19, teens develop physical, emotional, and sexual maturity while also establishing an individual identity apart from their family (Cleveland Clinic, n.d.). These teen years are indeed a challenging time for adolescent kids as they go through the physical changes of puberty and the emotional transformation that comes with it. In some cases, severe mental health conditions may even emerge (VeryWell Family & Morin, LCSW, 2019).

If you feel stressed in your work, so are your teens. They may be juggling pressures while simultaneously exploring relationships, tastes, lifestyles, and behaviors. Teen life is often a time of increasing pressures at school and in college when your youths need to make decisions about careers, work, or training. Things like this are stressful to teenagers. They may have entered the portal to a potentially exciting period in their lives – with many new opportunities opening up and personal choices to make. Still, all these can be overwhelming and confusing to them.

At this point, a teenager is idealistic and often finds themselves impatient and at odds with the adult world. They tend to believe that they have all the answers that most adults think they don't know. While things like this can be irritating, both you and your teen should discuss them so you can explore each other's beliefs rather than ignore what your teens believe in or put down their ideas. It is a matter of knowing them more and finding out whom they are apart from how you know them and what they believe in.

It is also during the puberty stage when many changes occur to a teen's physical body. They grow rapidly in weight and height. And as their sexual organ is developing, the body's production of sexual hormones soars. Such changes affect a teenager's behavior and attitude and can lead to mood swings. It is normal but can sometimes be confusing and frightening to both you and your kids.

During your child's teenage stage, you have this feeling that your child is suddenly slipping away from your control and transforming into someone not typical of them. They are becoming more distant and spending more time with peers than staying at home with their family. However, these changes are part of the essential process of moving toward independence. If you think there is something you can do to prevent your child from going through this, then you're mistaken. You have been through this, and so they must go through it the way you did.

Suppose you are trying to cure your child's behavior. In that case, there is no right prescription for this as each of your teenage kids has a different personality, a unique individual that needs particular advice. It is the reason why you need to communicate differently with your adolescent kids. It's not the same as when you communicate with younger children. If you are not aware of the appropriate communication style to use with them, you are more likely to get stressed or engage in conflict.

Every family and every teenager is unique and knowing how to respond to the needs of your teens is not always easy. There is no one-size-fits-all solution to every issue that worries you regarding your teens, and it can help you in your parenting of these youths to reflect on how you interact with them.

As the parents of these teens, you are the significant influencer in their lives and can shape their values and aspirations. Your impact on them, including your ability to develop them to ensure their bright future, will be molded by your own experience, strength, and limitations.

It is best to offer your teen empathy rather than judgment so you can continue to guide them and keep the relationship intact. It is not an easy process but understanding the teen's mind will help you have an easy transition.

Teenage years can indeed be challenging for many families as young people may develop values, beliefs, and ideas different from yours. While this is a normal process of moving towards independence, still, you may struggle with how much autonomy you should allow them.

Parents, especially mothers, are expected to perform a more significant role in supervising their children. However, some have their own business or career to focus on and lack time to be with them, so they feel guilty that their absence accounts for the lack of proper parental supervision.

As parents, you are protective of your kids, and because of this, you tend to be more aware of the many dangers looming around your kids and waiting for chances to prey on them. Most often, you would tell them not to do this or that without bothering to understand how they would respond to our orders. You may be unaware of the emotional impact that your words have on them, and as a result, you usually end up arguing or even fighting.

As parents, you are used to seeing your kids believing every word you say and obeying every order you give them. However, you fail to realize that this is where a significant transition in your children's life occurs as they enter their adolescent stage. Haven't we all been there before? Haven't we all gone through the same rebellious stage when we see our parents on the other side of the camp instead of joining us? We should have realized it sooner, but could it be that adulthood has this same effect on us?

It is at this stage when generation clashes start between parents and teenage children (familyeducation.com, 2017).

Communication issues often emerge as the primary cause of these clashes. You constantly complain of your kids being so REASONABLE, to which your teenage son or daughter would often say, "it's because parents are usually TOO UNREASONABLE!"

While communication plays a vital role in creating troubles between parents and teens, you can also use it as an effective tool in settling issues to improve your relationship with them. Only by having good relationships with your kids can you create awareness in them and help them understand why you behave the way you do. Conversely, with good communication and relationships with your teens, you can also see how they view things that you often neglect to see.

About the Author

My name is Kathy Wynne, a mother of four wonderful kids – two young boys and two young adult women.

Having graduated with an Accounting degree from UMUC, I used what I have learned from school to break into the business world and had been a proprietor for 20 years.

Despite my business success, I am still a mother who also wants to secure my kids' future. However, I am aware that it's not easy to raise kids even when you have almost everything that money can buy. Unlike business, kids, especially those approaching teens, have their ideas, beliefs, personality, and behavior challenges to handle. And since I'm not always around to see how they spend their time in school and even after classes, I can't help worrying over them.

I wrote this book to help parents like me navigate the tough times of dealing with their teenage sons and daughters. Having two teenagers of my own, I had experienced it, and we learned much from each other as we openly discussed and shared our issues and experiences. In my business, I have met many parents who shared with me their pains and problems. I feel that it's my responsibility to share what I have learned with you, to ease your pains, and to help you ensure that your kids can have a bright future ahead because of your support. My passion is helping you raise up a new generation of happy, healthy, and successful children.

This book will guide and advise parents on addressing common issues that parents would like to know more about regarding their teenage kids to truly understand and relate to them better and help them prepare their future for success. It won't be answering all the questions you have in mind but will get you, at least, a step closer to understanding your teenage son or daughter. Reading this book will provide you with a number of benefits but not limited to:

- ➲ Securing your teens against wrong peers.
- ➲ Knowing how to initiate conversations with teens to strengthen relations with them.
- ➲ Teaching them how to effectively encourage your teens to study and do their school work.
- ➲ Helping them understand why they need to follow house rules.
- ➲ Safeguarding your teens against the bad effects of social media and the internet in general.
- ➲ Giving awareness on the dangers and consequences of drugs and alcohol·
- ➲ Teaching your teens about healthy and unhealthy relationships, dating, and the consequence of early pregnancy.
- ➲ Providing your kids with budget awareness, money, management skills, and developing in them the right mindset for success.

While writing this book, I realized that nothing is more important than investing in your child's future while preparing and giving them love, advice, time, and guidance.

All information you get from here are real-life experiences, proven and tested to provide you with the essential conversation skills you need that will make a difference in your teenage son or daughter's life. Sharing with your teens the best lessons you have learned in life and from this book can be the best legacy you can give them.

Chapter 1

HOW TO START IMPORTANT CONVERSATIONS

When your children enter the adolescent stage, this is the time communication blocks occur between parents and teens. However, keeping the communication channel open will help you sort out any communication difficulties with your teenager to maintain a positive relationship. At this point, you need to consider the importance of essential topics with them, and the way you relate to them every day will determine if it will be easy or hard to sort out key issues. Communication is the key for parents to connect and have a good relationship. It is one of the most influential factors in their children's future and making decisions.

If you don't act carefully, it is easy to get locked into unhelpful forms of communication like nagging and criticizing, which can end up in constant bickering and arguments with your teens. Although your teenage children need your guidance, the boundaries you draw, and the authority you hold, you have to be strategic in getting these across to your kids.

The way you converse with your teens may be quite different than when dealing with rebellious kids and those who are naturally obedient and respectful. Let them know that you are interested and watchful of their activities because you care. It is important that they should know you will be on your side even though you and your teen may not see things eye to eye at all times. To deal with your teenagers, you need to keep an open line of communication, which requires communication skills and the emotional resilience to offer your help despite the indifference and opposition.

IMPROVING YOUR
COMMUNICATION SKILLS

By equipping yourself with the necessary communication skills, you can lessen the level of indifference and opposition from your teenage son or daughter.

Teenager's behavior often makes it difficult to accept how they are, which is also why a communication gap can develop and threaten your relationship with your kids.

You may not always be able to change your teenager without getting into a fight with them. Still, you can control your behavior, actions, and responses – especially your words, which often cause damage to the relationship you are trying hard to build. How you behave towards your children affects their behavior towards you. By improving your communication skills, you can keep an open communication channel that will serve as your way to reach out to them.

Consider this guide on how to maintain open communication with your teenagers as they progress through those difficult teen years.

HOW TO KEEP AN OPEN COMMUNICATION

When trying to start a conversation with your teenage son or daughter, always choose a good time. It is best to talk about anything without pressure or agenda, as random talks tend to flow naturally. You may bring up some topics to share with them while hanging out together, doing chores like washing clothes or dishes, or while in the car on your way to the grocery store. However, be sensitive, especially to any changes in your teen's reaction or responses. Are they willing to engage in this type of conversation with you? If they are busy with something else or have had a bad day, wait for a better opportunity to have a conversation with them.

Although there is nothing wrong with asking your teenagers questions like, "How was your day?" it still sounds mechanical if you do it daily or every time your kid arrives from school. As a parent, you can do much more to engage with your teens, and times like this are precious for both of you, making your conversation positive and productive.

Many would assume that as children move into the teenage years, they find their families less critical, as their attention is now more focused on their peers. As a parent, you know that this is the time when they need you more, although it may be true that the relationship is shifting during your child's teenage years. When they are still very young, your role in their life is to care for and nurture them, but you will realize that your child is becoming an equal as they grow.

During the adolescent stage, teenagers are going through an emotional roller coaster, and their parents and family are their sources of emotional support. As they become more mature, their relationship with their family becomes more stable and robust.

It's natural for teens to become moody and distant, so it is hard to start a conversation with them, but it does not mean they need you less. Your child will always love you even though hormonal changes cause changes in their behavior and attitudes. They want you to continue caring and spending some time in a conversation.

Maintaining open communication with your teenage children must not be difficult. There are ways to consider in keeping communications lines open with your teens.

- ⮑ Avoid nagging,
- ⮑ Using "I" is better than "You,"
- ⮑ Take time to listen,
- ⮑ Show empathy,
- ⮑ Treat them as an equal,
- ⮑ Be a good role model,
- ⮑ Avoid being judgmental,
- ⮑ Show your kids your appreciation,
- ⮑ Show them your love,
- ⮑ Draw boundaries,
- ⮑ Reward them with praises,
- ⮑ Give them the freedom to decide,
- ⮑ Understand and provide help only when needed.

WHY DO YOUR TEENS NEED YOU MORE

When your teenage son or daughter is experiencing rapid physical and emotional changes, they feel confused and don't know where they fit in. While they don't want you to treat them like little kids, they are afraid when they think you are not giving them your attention. While they undergo this stage in their life, it can cause you both some stress. Therefore, you must support each other as you go through such challenges.

Remember that your child still finds your family a secure emotional base in terms of emotion where they feel loved and accepted regardless of what they're going through. So, you must build and support their confidence, optimism, self-belief, and identity.

Setting family rules, boundaries, and standards of behavior give your teenage child a sense of consistency and predictability while protecting them from acquiring lousy behavior like the use of alcohol and drugs, as well as smoking. Supportive and closer ties within the family will also prevent mental issues like depression and can go a long way to training your child to be a caring, considerate, and well-balanced adult.

TIPS ON BUILDING FAMILY RELATIONSHIPS WITH TEENAGERS

Almost everyone, regardless of age, enjoys talking and having others listen to them – from toddlers to adults. Effective communication is significantly the basis for developing healthy and mutually rewarding parent-children and husband-wife relationships. Consider the following in building a relationship with your teenage son or daughter.

Make Family Mealtime an Opportunity for Good Conversations

You can make mealtimes especially encouraging for your family by promoting a climate that fosters smooth and open communication. It will help your kids create a positive view of themselves and the world they live in and develop a positive outlook on life. Make it your goal to let everyone think of mealtime as a communication time – a time when you can talk with your children, especially teens, and obtain feedback from them. It can also be your chance to nurture them. Consider getting rid of all forms of distractions like cellphones, televisions, or any unfinished activities.

Always remember that children need adults, especially their parents, to eat with them. Regardless of how nutritious a meal is, a meal is of little importance to kids who want their parents' attention. When you eat together with your kids at mealtimes, you're not only feeding healthy foods but also serving as a role model for their food choices. So, ensure that your mealtimes are always exciting and fun for everyone to achieve your communication goal.

Schedule Family Outings

A family that spends time together builds more trust, which is an essential factor in all relationships. Try setting aside time for family outings. Spending a relaxing time with your teenage kids can help create a strong bond and sense of togetherness. It can also be your chance to learn more about your kid's strengthened values.

Because of too much electronic distraction, parents are looking for ways to cope with them. One way is through scheduling family outings to encourage family bonding and spending more time with each other. The challenge to keep a family, particularly maintaining a solid bond with your child as they become teenagers, is not easy. Nonetheless, it is a vital aspect of modern parenting.

You can involve your teenage son or daughter in planning family activities. You can hold a family meeting to brainstorm activities for everybody to enjoy. You may want to consider the following in planning your family outings:

- ➲ Planning a holiday vacation,
- ➲ Having a picnic at the park,

- Going swimming at a beach resort,
- Go on an excursion,
- Going shopping, watching a movie, or dining out.

Take Time to Have One-On-One With Your Teen

Taking the time to have a one-on-one with your teen keeps you connected. Those bonding moments are quite an experience for your child, which they will cherish forever. You may watch a movie together or dine out or have lunch together. You may also spend the weekend redecorating your house or reorganizing your child's room. Anything that interests both of you is worth doing to spend those moments with each other. Remember, these activities don't need to be planned all the time. They happen spontaneously. If you haven't tried this out in the past, your child may need a little encouragement. If you have a relationship issue with your child, you may consider inviting their best friend. Spend more time with your teen to build more rapport and try finding out what activities you both enjoy most.

Acknowledge Your Child's Accomplishments

One incredible way to nourish and encourage your child's progress in performance and many other areas in life is by celebrating their success. By praising them in their everyday achievements and achieving milestones – either big or small, you are unlocking one of the most powerful tools to connect and support your child in their continuous development.

Parents need to praise both the effort and accomplishment of their children to realize that life is not always perfect. Holding on to these achievements and efforts can spark your children's inner desire to do their best, not just because they want their parents to give them praise but because they have set their standard of self-worth.

Create and Maintain Family Traditions

You may choose to create and maintain family traditions in addition to routines and family rituals to help you and your child set aside a regular schedule to be together and enjoy each other's company. You may enjoy cooking together on weekends, having a picnic at the park, or scheduling a movie night with pizza.

Never underestimate the significance of family traditions. Family traditions you created around mealtimes like praying together last a lifetime. There is always a good chance that your children will carry on this tradition when they have their own family later.

Some families have these family traditions because they have significant meanings to them while establishing special bonds between parent-child and sibling-sibling. But what makes these traditions important is that they create positive experiences and memories for everyone by giving them a sense of belonging. It nurtures family connections in a way that's significant to every family member.

Family traditions, likewise, help your teens understand who they are and their importance to the family. Traditions further create a connection for those that give them a sense of uniqueness, contributing to higher self-esteem and enhanced well-being. It is because children, especially teens, find comfort and security in things that are predictable and consistent.

Assign Them Household Responsibilities

Assigning your child tasks gives them the feeling that they are making a significant contribution to the family. As they see their obvious involvement, they are more likely to value their family even while facing their challenges in life during the adolescent stage.

Get them involved in household chores – preparing, cooking, cleaning, gardening, taking care of younger children, and running errands. A family that labors together is more likely to understand family values.

Make Sure Your Teen Observes Family Rules

To instill discipline in the family, parents need to establish rules that are bound to be followed by children. Because teen children are often defiant, these rules aim to realign their behavior and keep them within bounds.

Conduct Family Meetings

Some families call for family meetings to settle issues that generally impact the whole family.

Family meetings are discussions involving every family member and are centered on a particular issue. However, family meetings are often about a topic related to a problem that the family is experiencing at the moment. You may also use family meetings to plan time together or prevent an issue from occurring. Such meetings provide family members a time to focus on the family. Considering the fast-paced and hectic lives many families lead, this is truly an essential part.

Family meetings can be in the form of one-time events or they can be held regularly. The family leader must be nonjudgmental when leading the discussion.

Family meetings are most effective if they are not limited to handling crises, asserting discipline, or assigning jobs. Other reasons for holding a family meeting could be:

- ⮡ Sharing information that affects family members,
- ⮡ Having fun together,
- ⮡ Planning weekly schedules or calendars so that everyone will know what they need to do or what commitments have been made,
- ⮡ Making family decisions about recreations, vacations, and other activities.

Seek Family Support When Needed

If you think that your family isn't connecting, you may seek support from family counselors or Parenting

Support Services to receive interventions from outside sources to enhance positive family functioning.

Parents can be more resourceful and practical problem solvers with support. They can likewise create a safe learning environment for their teens at home to develop emotional, cognitive, and behavioral strength. Parent support groups are designed to build, strengthen, and support parents' relationship capabilities, so they are better equipped in providing a quality relationship.

HELPFUL TIPS WHEN CONVERSING WITH TEENS

Whether a conversation is casual or challenging, it can be an opportunity for parents to guide their children. It will be easier to communicate effectively with your kids if you start with a plan. A plan to improve your communication skills should take into consideration when, where, or how to approach significant conversations.

Here are some helpful conversation tips you can use to guide you in your conversation with your teens.

Converse with Your Teen as Often and as Early as You Can

Having a conversation with your teens helps develop brain growth, creates a stronger bond and healthier attachments. Start having open discussions with your kids early and as often as you can. So by the time they hit the adolescence stage, they will find it easy and comfortable to talk with you. Once you can have your child's complete trust and confidence, having established a conversation habit will help you walk them through the difficult stage of adolescence.

Be Mindful of Yourself

If you have a voiced an opinion on some matters, check yourself before having a conversation about it with your teens. Teenagers are very much aware of what you're going to say, and if they think that you won't accept others' opinions on the matter, they are most likely to avoid engaging with you.

Restrain Yourself from Extreme Emotions

It is essential to create a peaceful environment while discussing some issues with your teens. When you aren't calm or tend to yell or overreact, you can't expect them to be at peace with you. The worst part is, they may block the conversation entirely.

It's always best to remain calm, listen, and react unless you have heard enough of their side. If you feel that the matter on hand is getting out of control, take a break and chill. You don't want your teens to lose their respect for you, and they are most likely to feel that way once you behave in an extreme way, contrary to their expectations.

Be Careful With Your Words

Your tone and choice of words are essential when dealing with your teens. Most teens feel they are also blamed because of the negative and accusatory tone that parents often use, like "Why can't you do better in anything?" Instead, you may say, "I know you can do better than this, so it frustrates me to see that you just don't care."

If your kids know how you feel, they might try to understand you.

Actively Listen to What Your Teen Tries to Tell You

Active listening is just as critical as talking to your child. Sometimes, it's even more effective to guide them in dealing with challenges instead of constantly offering solutions through suggestions. However, active listening is a skill that you need to learn, and it requires practice. In a most open and honest communication, you should allow your kids to do most of the talking so you can get a complete grasp of how they think and feel. The bottom line is to let them know that you understand them and what they're going through, for you have been in their shoes before.

Try Seeing Their Point of View

Because your teens look upon you with respect, they need your parental approval. When it comes to essential topics like going out with the wrong people, try not to judge, preach, or lecture them. If you do, your kids may avoid having a conversation with you.

Telling your kids directly that you don't like their friends and avoiding them is like telling them you don't trust their judgment, and this will make them feel that they have lost your confidence and tend to absorb all the negative messages you're sending. Why not allow them to guide you on what they need instead? Try seeing things the way your teens see them.

Choose a Peaceful Environment Suitable for Talking

Know the kind of environment that suits your teens' temperament or mood. Are they mellow when there is music or total silence in the background? It would be best not to trigger negative emotions in your kids when you have a conversation about significant issues in their life and success.

If others are listening and you confront them, they will most likely retaliate by not listening or discussing things with you.

Converse Privately

When bringing something up to talk about with your teens, make sure you don't do it in public as it could lead to a public outburst. You may get your kids in on the conversation while doing something together, like household chores. It's easy to talk about something at random, like when washing dishes or doing laundry. You may also talk about it when driving him to school.

Avoid Ganging Up on Your Teen

Parenting is a partnership which is probably why we often want to talk with our kids together, especially when it involves significant issues. However, doing it this way can make your child feel like you're ganging up on them. So, consider only one of you to have this conversation with your teen, depending on the topic. Just agree beforehand on whatever decision will be made so you won't end up having disagreements.

Actively Engage in a Conversation with Your Teen

While having a conversation with your kid, make sure you have your full attention on them. Avoid all forms of distractions – no call, no texts, or any physical intervention. Make your kid feel that at this time, you are there for them alone and whatever it is that they'll be sharing with you is of utmost importance as they are to you.

Ask Open-Ended Questions

Make sure that you don't sound accusatory when having a conversation with your kids. Avoid asking direct questions like, "Is your friend a drug addict?"

Instead, you may say, "Are you aware that your friend is into drugs?"

By using open-ended questions, you will learn more from their answers. Encourage your teen to give their opinions instead of directly giving your own and forcing them to accept them as facts. Most teens will show open defiance and even tell a lie to defend themselves if they feel they are being judged.

Let Them Know You're Not Perfect

It won't hurt to show your kids that you are vulnerable and can commit mistakes. Often parents make the mistake of behaving like someone high and mighty before their kids, leading to a communication gap. Showing your kids that you, like them, are also vulnerable to commit mistakes will help them understand that you can fully relate to them because you have committed the same mistake before. It is essential to let them know the lessons you have learned from such mistakes so they can avoid them and won't need to experience the consequences.

Find Opportunities to Teach Your Teen

When directly confronted about their behavior, teens have this tendency to either tell a lie or avoid getting into a confrontation. A direct approach is sometimes unavoidable, but if you want to teach your kids lessons in life without offending them, you may take advantage of opportunities like discussing films you have watched together or notice messages behind some music. You must also be aware of some trends in fashion, hairstyles, lifestyles, etc. Take time to be mindful of what's going on around you- primarily through social media. You can always find opportunities to use as conversation starters and inject lessons you want them to learn.

Carry Your Conversation Over to the Future

It is vital that your conversation with your kid is a continuing process and not occasional events in your life. It is why you must start having easy and open conversations with them while they are still young, so this can become a habit – a part of their routine as well as yours. If you have your work and don't have much time to spend, you can let them know that you have your communication channels open for them if they need you.

Chapter 2

WHAT ABOUT SCHOOL AND HOMEWORK?

*W*hen your child arrives home from school, it seems normal to ask, "How's school?" to which your teenage child usually answers, "It's alright."

To answer this, you expect your kid to sum their whole day or give you at least a few details on what happened at school.

However, most kids, especially teenagers, feel that their experiences in school are private, and they don't want to share them. Doing such is a normal part of their development as they shape their identities and social worlds. Despite these, your child still needs to know that you're always there when they are ready to share their experiences with you.

Once you can completely relate to your child's feelings about school, you can see potential problems before they gets big. This way, you can work together with your child to overcome challenges. Discussing school issues, like projects, school events, or about friends, will give you the chance to express your family values about things like teamwork, empathy, respect for others, gratitude, etc.

A GLIMPSE ON
YOUR CHILD'S EXPERIENCE

Parents tend to express their worries when it comes to what kind of student their child is. Most of them feel helpless or embarrassed since they are uncertain of how to help them in their education. Others don't know how to make their teenagers relax and balance themselves as they become obsessed with being perfect. Because of this, they eventually become tired of what they are doing as a parent or guardian.

On the other hand, teenagers also suffer from stress to meet everyone's expectations, especially their family. It can result in something that will make them think that their goals are impossible, eventually making them shut down. Other teenagers' psyche allows them to raise their hurdle a notch higher, resulting in exhaustion. If you're a parent and clueless about the right things to do, listed below are some tried and tested tips that might be able to help you out.

WAYS TO HANDLE CONVERSATIONS WITH YOUR TEEN ABOUT SCHOOL AND HOMEWORK

#1 – Assist Your Teen in Finding Their Purpose in Life

School and homework might be more meaningful if your teen has an authentic purpose to fulfill. For example, it would be advantageous for them to talk to their Spanish-speaking friends if they study the Spanish language. They will also become healthy if they involve themselves in their school's sports clubs and extracurriculars. Having a purpose will also help them realize their dreams in the future. Additionally, you can also talk to them about how their academic studies today will impact their future goals, making them well-aware of your opinions as a parent. Keep in mind, however, to share advice when they ask for it.

#2 – Help Your Teens Discover Their Learning Needs and Styles

There are different learning needs and styles, so letting your child discover theirs is very important for their progress. For example, if they learn faster through observing videos or visual aids, provide research tools that support their preference. It might not be feasible in their school due to systematic reasons, so your strategy should be done at home as additional help. Some schools, however, allow recording apps and typing notes, so make sure to clarify those with their teachers first.

#3 – Encourage Self-Advocacy

Instead of self-sufficiency, teach your child the importance of self-advocacy, especially when voicing their needs and seeking help from their teachers. Discuss appropriate times for these things, e.g., before or after class, group study times, etc. Support their critical thinking and self-awareness capabilities by providing them with helpful role plays and practice as needed. As teens voice their needs without worries, they steadily build trust and safety in their learning environments.

#4 – Incorporate Conversations Into Family Routines

Systems and routines help people to stay on track and stick to their personal goals. Establish homework routines such as no screen time while doing assignments unless required, having breaks after 20-30 minutes, dinner at seven o'clock, and so on. That way, you can still emphasize the importance of having rest even while studying. Encourage your teen to use timers to increase accountability and promote self-efficiency. As a parent, you might have to readjust those routines to adhere to the school's system, making sure to apply the necessary adjustment accordingly to prevent mishaps.

#5 – Go for Growth, Not for Perfection

It would be better for children who tend to have perfectionist tendencies if they do not exert additional academic pressure. Overdoing it can push them to overwork. It can continue until the pressure becomes too overwhelming for them. When this happens, they might give up on everything, especially school. So instead of forcing them to study too much, teach them the importance of growth instead. Make sure to celebrate every small victory and improvement on their side to motivate them more.

#6 – Help Them Make Better Choices

It will be helpful for teens if you support their activities outside of school as long as these activities aren't harmful. Encourage them to decide for themselves when it involves their interests and passions to boost their self-confidence. Opportunities like creative writing, video games, sports, study groups, or even church and other community groups may do the trick. Always express interest in their motivation in joining, especially if it motivates and helps them manage new commitments.

Always keep in mind that a fail-safe strategy for these kinds of things does not exist, which require you to adjust accordingly for the sake of your teen's well-being.

WAYS TO HELP YOUR
TEEN THRIVE IN HIGH SCHOOL

Parents have a very crucial role in helping their teenage children succeed in school and life as a whole. Teenagers may want to try being independent at times but still need a little support and guidance from everyone, especially their parents. In this stage, teens need their parents more than ever, even during their high school life.

)w are ways to help them succeed in high

#1 – rarticipate in **Parents-Teachers Meetings**

Teenage students do better whenever they see their parents support their academic efforts. Hence, attending parent-teacher meetings is the best way to get to know your teen's teachers and their expectations. During these times, teachers might discuss programs that need the whole class' involvement and essential matters that parents and guardians need to be informed of. Additionally, attending these conferences helps parents stay informed, though nowadays, such meetings in high school are primarily concerned about teens' behavioral problems or failing grades. Keep in mind, however, that parents can always request meetings with teachers, the principal, school administration, and other staff anytime during the school year.

#2 –Explore School Vicinity and Website

Being aware of the school's entire physical layout can help you relate with your teen whenever you talk to them about the school day. It will be advantageous to know your teen's classroom and other areas, like the gym, central office, infirmary, canteen, and special classrooms.

Additionally, if the school has an official website, you can also find other helpful information such as staff, special day events, examination days, periodic grading assessment days, and much more. Some teachers even have their websites and email addresses posted on the school's main site. Having access to these resources can further help your kids through the provision of digital textbooks, work assignments, and other resources.

#3 – Provide Your Teen a Distraction-Free Zone to Study

High school years are preparation for college entrance. During your child's high school years, homework gets more intense, and grades become more critical. Teens learn from many aspects of their lives, including school and extracurricular activities, along with social and side hustles.

It is necessary to make sure that your child is free from all forms of distraction, including TV and other electronic gadgets. Would you mind providing them with a quiet place to study well and sufficient materials and supplies they need?

Regularly monitor how they are doing in school and if there are things they need. Also, check on their class schedule to see that they're not overloaded and help them stick to their study and homework schedule. If they need help with their projects, provide them with the resources and encourage them to do it independently and not do it for them.

#4 – Take Care of Your Teen's Energy Needs

Attending school with an empty stomach is a no-no for students, especially teenagers, since it hampers their concentration and ability to learn. Additionally, having breakfast before going to school will give your kids enough energy to last until lunchtime. You can enhance your teen's learning abilities and attention span by providing foods rich in fiber and protein along with whole-grain foods with low added sugar content. You can also add nuts, fresh fruits, or a peanut butter sandwich. Aside from that, teens also need at least eight to ten hours of sleep to maintain a sharp memory.

#5 – Help Them Acquire Organizational Skills

Making teens learn and master organizational skills enables them to focus and concentrate on whatever they do. However, this is usually taught in school, so it would be better to learn directly from their parents. Creating a calendar to write reminders can help them recognize upcoming deadlines for their projects and school activities. be sure to keep them stay informed and reminded about their non-academic obligations, e.g., laundry day, general cleaning day, etc.

#6 – Assist Them in Their Studies

When your teen has difficulty in learning academics, break down their tasks into smaller ones. That way, they won't be overwhelmed and crammed whenever their examination days come. Teach them to juggle multiple subjects effectively through careful planning and organization. Make quizzes regarding the subject area they're studying, focusing on troublesome or hard-to-remember areas that might appear on their actual test. And always remember that having enough rest is better than cramming.

#7 – Be Knowledgeable of School Policies and Procedures

Bullying issues are alarmingly common among teens on school campuses around the world (Rivara, 2016). Different countries have different rules and likewise, schools differ in their policies and disciplinary actions for students with behavioral issues. Schools usually cite these policies inside student handbooks and during orientation days. These policies include proper dress codes, acceptable language, and attendance. It may also involve particular actions regarding juvenile delinquency issues like bullying, vandalism, cheating, gang/fraternity/sorority involvements, or other groups not recognized by the school. Your teen must know what's expected from them while studying as well as the consequences they might face whenever those requirements aren't met.

8 – Participate in Your Teen's School Activities

High school life is often when your kids prefer to be treated like adults, and they are embarrassed if their friends see that you still treat them as your little kid.

Unlike when they were still much younger than they are now, they don't want you to get involved as much as possible. However, there are school events and activities that need your presence and involvement. Follow your teen's cues to determine when you should stay behind the scenes and when you have your presence felt. Make them feel that you don't want to cause them embarrassment, but you are always there when needed.

- ➲ You can get involved by attending Parents-Teachers Association.
- ➲ Attending important events like competitions, sports events, concerts, plays, etc.
- ➲ Sponsoring some school activities.
- ➲ Organizing some fundraising activities in support of some school programs.

#9 – Monitor Their Attendance

If your teen suddenly gets sick, such as suffering from fever, nausea, vomiting, or diarrhea, they should take a sick day off. Otherwise, they need to attend school since having to catch up with everything after being absent can be pretty troublesome, particularly on their side. Taking note of their school attendance also keeps you informed of other troubling matters such as issues with classmates or teachers, low grades, cutting classes, challenging assignments, tardiness, and school bullying. The school can work with their families accordingly and limit their workload to stay on track for teens with chronic health issues.

#10 –A Regular Conversation About School Means a Lot

High school life is the most eventful period in one's life. Needless to say, as a parent, you better expect something to happen on a daily basis. Hence, it would be better for parents to talk to teens about their school from time to time. If you don't receive any news or think there might be something wrong or missing about what your teen told you, you can take the necessary measures.

YOUR TEEN MAY
HATE DOING HOMEWORK

Everyone is unique in their way, especially teens. Some of them are naturally and easily motivated, and some aren't. Some of them keep up with their school's requirements (e.g., regular attendance, doing homework, etc.), while others seem to find it hard to go to school at all. If you're a parent of a teen who seems to find it challenging to attend school, it might be somewhat frustrating on your side. However, instead of lashing out, experts recommend that you do the things below to prevent yourself from losing your cool. Here's how.

Find Out the Problem's Root Cause

If your teen suddenly refuses to do their homework or attend school all of a sudden, try not to think that they're just doing it to defy you as their parent. It is more likely that underlying issues prevent them from doing those, such as stress or bullying. Depression, learning disabilities, anxieties, and even advanced classes can contribute to this problem, creating too much pressure for your teen. It is impossible for them to maintain concentration when this happens. As a result, many teens give up schooling once they start seeing low or failing grades in their class cards. It is also helpful if you, as a parent, talk to their teachers to check out their thoughts and perspectives about the situation.

Ask Your Teen for More Information

Not all teens refuse to talk about their school affairs and issues. For those who do, make sure that you speak to them about it. Take a deep breath first and assess the situation, whatever the problem is. Don't try starting the conversation with accusations, blame games, or threats. Instead, ask them with a sense of curiosity and help them uncover the issue without exerting unnecessary pressure on them. So whenever you receive a letter or notice from the teacher or school principal regarding your teen's behavior, try to calm yourself down first.

Find Effective Solutions to the Issue

Once you get wind of your teen's problem, make sure to brainstorm a list of possible solutions to the given issue or situation. At this moment, you may need to predict likely consequences for each action taken, both positive and negative. Teens should be encouraged not to underestimate themselves and come up with as many solutions as possible. This creative process helps generate better solutions.

Once done, narrow the entire list together with your teen. Sometimes, doing homework needs a creative solution depending on your teen's personality. Some of them like to finish everything before going home. Others want to rest before doing their homework, and still, others need a tutor to help them out with their lessons. Make sure to apply the perfect solution to provide them with confidence to overcome the issue.

Set Rules and Expectations

Some teens fail their classes or refuse to attend school because they do not have healthy study habits, making them seem inferior compared to their classmates. In that case, you might as well establish rules and expectations on them. Make sure to set a study time for them wherein they are forbidden to do anything else during that time, such as playing games and watching TV unless necessary. If your teen is fairly responsible with homework most of the time, allowing them to face the consequences of a bad grade or detention whenever they refuse to do homework might help. On the other hand, for teens, who still refuse to do homework even if there are no underlying problems, it would be helpful to establish a reward system for them to get motivated.

Whenever a parent faces a school problem regarding their teen, they must keep themselves calm and open-minded. Tempting parent techniques such as nagging and lecturing are harmful to the parent-child relationship, especially when profanities are included. When done incorrectly, reward systems can be considered bribing and may instill a "What's in it for me" attitude to your child in the long run. Once you discover the problem, make sure that you apply the most effective solution to it as quickly as possible to prevent mishaps shortly.

HOW TO DEAL
WITH FAILING GRADES

Dealing with failing grades can be frustrating, both on the parent and student sides. For the student, especially teens, failing grades could mean difficulty getting into the university or college of their choice, lower GPA, or even an inability to graduate. For the parents, on the other hand, it could mean that they failed as a parent or lesser bragging rights during family-relative gatherings. When this happens, it is easy for teens to get discouraged, eventually giving up on school when left unchecked.

If your teen is failing or has failed their class already, make sure to take action before the situation worsens. Listed below are some of the things you should do as soon as possible.

Identify the Issue

As a parent, always keep yourself calm whenever your teen hands out their class report cards to you, no matter what the situation is. Failing this first and foremost task could result in your teen hiding their report cards from you.

Discuss the Issue With the Teacher

Your teen might not like this but, as a parent, it is your responsibility to talk with their teachers whenever something like this happens to them. There are times when your teen fails a class due to negligence or failure to do tasks such as projects, assignments, etc. They might also not pay much attention while in class, or they might be missing a lot of important work or subject-related matters. Make sure to ask the teachers and clarify whether issues such as these happen to your teen.

Work It Out Together With Your Teens

Next, if you notice that your teen has a failing grade or might be in danger of failing a class subject, sit down and discuss the problem with them. Ask your teen about the probable reasons why they failed or might fail their class. The reason behind the failure may be one or more of these problems:

Classes Might Be Difficult

Whether we accept it or not, one might excel in one subject and have difficulty in another. It is also the same with your teen, and it's simply inevitable. To prevent this, you might also help them out in that subject or hire a tutor to teach them well about it.

Skipping/Not Doing Homework

Doing homework is a school requirement since it also means additional grades or credits for the student. If your teen skips this part just because they don't feel like doing it, failing a class will be inevitable.

Low Test or Examination Score

Tests and exams are the main components behind a student's grades, homework, projects, and recitation. If your teen has low grades here, it will also affect their overall grades.

Absences or Tardiness

If your teen is frequently late or absent because of illness and other possible reasons, it can severely affect their grades in school.

Investigate/Observe Thoroughly

There might be a chance that your teen may not tell you the real reason behind the failure of his grades or absences in some classes. Usually, if your teen refuses to attend a school or a class subject, the chances are that they might not like to see a particular person. It might be a student of another class – that is, if they have joint classes. Sometimes, it could even be the subject teacher. It is possible that your teen kid is being bullied, which usually involves physical violence. Make sure to take the proper action when addressing them.

Once you determine the issue, make sure to help your teen out in solving it. For example, if your teen finds it difficult to catch up with the lesson during classes, make sure to let them take supplementary but not stressful tasks at home. If they don't understand something about their homework, check it out and, with some online assistance, help them out with it.

Some teens find it difficult to concentrate whenever they are hungry, so make sure that they eat breakfast before going to school. Don't forget to prepare food for their lunchtime as well.

DEALING WITH UNMOTIVATED TEENS AND TEENS WHO LIE

Adolescence, as people know, is a time of constant and unpredictable change. As teens grow and develop, it is not unusual for them to not know what to do with their lives, leading to impulsive and constantly changing decisions. However, if the teen lacks direction, it is not normal.

WHAT TO DO WITH UNMOTIVATED TEENS

Even though their hopes and dreams are not well-defined, teens should still be able to express them. Some teens are enthusiastic and seem to know what they want, while others seem disinterested in their future. The latter may appear unmotivated and lack concrete plans. When this happens, it is up to their parents to help them find their way. When left unchecked, this could result in longer parenting times compared to what is expected.

In the United States alone, about sixty percent of the parents still provide continuous financial support to their children despite having graduated.

Inspire Teens

No one can force children and teens to become motivated except themselves. If parents act pushy or domineering towards them, they will either become more irresponsible or rebellious. You can try the tips listed below if you find difficulties in inspiring your teen.

Discover and Nurture Your Teen's Interest

The best way to get teens inspired is to tap into their natural and personal interests. Consider your teen's strengths and weaknesses which will help them connect their talents with their future. For example, if they like music, help them get a part-time job at a music store or studio. Make sure to connect their interests with personal and real-world experiences.

Help Find Solutions to Their Worries

There are times wherein teens feel overwhelmed by the demands of becoming an adult. When this happens, you can talk to them about the responsibilities of an adult, orienting and making them learn about it as soon as possible. Discuss the types of work they want to do, help them in making impressive resumes and work portfolios, and encourage them to attend a job interview.

Be an Inspiration

It is natural for children to look up to their parents as an example or role model. So if you want your teens to become motivated, make sure that you show motivation in yourself. It is useless for a parent to talk to their teens about motivation who is unmotivated themselves.

Help Teens Find the Right Career for Them

According to experts, teens are more likely to graduate, improve their academic performance, and pursue goals if they find a career that excites them. The only problem here is that most of them do not know the requirements of different career types, which negatively affects their self-esteem even before they try. If a career test is available, make sure to let them determine the careers that are possible for them to pursue. There are lots of possibilities, so make sure to help them find the right job for them.

Orient Teens on Financial Independence

Once your teen reaches high school level, it would be helpful for them if they learn that not all things should be spoon-fed to them. If they want something for themselves, you can suggest that they do some part-time jobs. Encourage them to budget their allowances, work, and save if they want something for themselves. If they still stay inside your home, do not encourage them to become a freeloader. Instead, please encourage them to help out in paying for food, lodging, and utilities. That way, they will become responsible and confident.

DEALING WITH A TEEN WHO LIES

Telling a lie is not uncommon for children. It is not unusual for children to lie to avoid punishment, protect their privacy, or even evade their responsibility. However, lying becomes a severe problem if they are starting to make stories just for the sake of covering up a more dangerous situation such as drug or alcohol use. So, whatever is the teen's reason behind lying, parents should take the matter seriously at all times.

Listed below are some helpful tips to address lying done by your teen.

Set a Good Example

Children tend to follow any example shown to them by their parents, regardless of whether it's good or bad. If the school asks you to volunteer in their activities, but you refuse by saying you are busy when you're not, you justify that it is okay to lie to your teen. Always keep in mind that you should always value honesty and truthfulness and apply it to your own life as a parent. That way, your children will live up to your shown example.

Set Clear Punishments for Lying

Children, especially teens, need to know you can't tolerate lying. Make sure to declare that lying in the family is a severe offense, and those who will commit the mistake of telling a lie will be subject to appropriate punishment. For example, if they lie about finishing their homework, they should be banned from phone and internet use for a week.

Explain the Possible Consequences of Lying

Children tend to have a limited understanding, especially when it comes to the consequences of their lies. To prevent those, it is helpful if you can explain that liars tend to face dire consequences. For example, if they tell a lie, it will affect them and the people around them. Would you please encourage them to be honest whenever possible since lying breaks the trust of people who believe in you?

Encourage Them to Make Better Choices

Whenever you find out that your child is lying to you, make sure not to give them a lecture for it. Instead, discuss the issue and let them explain themselves while keeping yourself calm. Once you find out the reason behind their lying, please encourage them to think of good alternatives to their decisions without telling a lie. That way, your children will not hesitate to communicate with you as much as possible. After all, who wants to talk to an angry person?

Lies tend to hurt people more than we think. It might be a simple issue for lying, but it is hurtful for those on the receiving end of the lie. Lies break trust, and once you break the trust, it is never easy to fix. Every time the liar's lies are found out, they need to deal with the angry people who have resentment towards them. It might cause people to turn away from them, eventually leaving themselves isolated in the process.

Having all these conversations with your teens about schools and education is significant to their success. Knowing that you care about their performances in school motivates your kids to do more and thrive for good performance to meet parents' expectations. Although other kids may find parents' intervention troubling when they feel they couldn't live up to their expectations, it's up to you to balance it. As a parent, it's best to guide your kids but not pressure them. That is why having a conversation - as in open communication is vital to eliminate whatever form of misunderstanding that threatens your relationship.

Chapter 3

CHOOSING THE RIGHT
FRIENDS FOR LONG-TERM
SUCCESS

*Y*ou may worry about your kids hanging out with the wrong crowd, get into trouble, and gaining bad influence. Choosing false friends can have a significant impact on your kid's success.

Before this happens, you may want to let your teenage son or daughter know why it is necessary to determine the right friends and how to choose them.

It is essential to guide your kids in choosing the right kind of people to befriend before it's too late. What if they are hanging out with toxic individuals? This kind of friendship can have an impact on your kids, not only for the time being. It can go beyond the present, affect their future, and hinder their success in life.

As early as possible, teach your kids how to recognize toxic friendships and how they must deal with friends that do them more harm than good. Suffering teenagers may tend toy hide the challenges they are facing and suffer in silence instead. Parents are usually the last to know.

WHAT A TOXIC FRIEND DOES

Here are some characteristics of a toxic friend that they must learn to spot as quickly as possible so they can get away from them before they can harm them. Share these ideas with your kids when you have the time to converse about them. It is better to provide them with this information as early as possible and before they get entangled with someone toxic. It would be difficult for you to communicate with your teenage son or daughter by that time.

A Toxic Friend Tends to Belittle You

Does your friend demean you regularly and make you feel miserable? Friends usually joke and tease each other, but think about it if the joking and teasing go below the belt. Good-natured teasing with you laughing about it isn't a toxic friendship. However, outright insults and subtle nagging tactics are signs that your friendship is an unhealthy one.

They Talk Behind Your Back

If you tell a supposed-to-be friend a secret and the following day everybody knows all the details, it only means the person can't be trusted, especially if you noticed that the person is relatively consistent in doing this.

Though there are times that people slip up and say things that they aren't supposed to say, toxic friends enjoy spilling out secrets even if you tell them to keep these things to themselves only. Sure enough, these friends don't care about your feelings.

They are Insincere in Their Apology

You call out your friend for their wrongdoings, but they don't take to heart what happened. They will give you a defensive "sorry" – the one with a "but" – the kind of apology that you know is non-apologetic. It only means that your friend doesn't care how their actions hurt your feelings.

You Feel Like You're Walking on Eggshells When You're Around Them

It's not that you should always have the ability to predict your friend's reactions. However, if your friend's response is harmful or abusive, be cautious. It's just reasonable that they should express their feelings without harming anyone, especially you, who trust them.

Let's say your friend got highly irritated and shouted at you because of a simple thing like forgetting to return their book. But after a while, she behaves as if nothing happened.

The point here is at least you should know how your friend will react in a particular situation. Otherwise, you will be walking on eggshells when you are hanging out with them.

You Feel Uncomfortable in Their Presence

When you spend time with your close friend, does it feel good, upsetting, or make you uneasy? If you think negatively every time you're with that friend and you feel relieved when they are gone or don't want to hang out with them again, check for other signs. It might be that you have that unsettled feeling because there's something wrong with the friendship.

Always Compares You to Someone Better

A friend that constantly points out your weak spots and makes you feel or implies that you are somehow less than others is not a good friend at all. Good friends recognize and appreciate their friends' unique traits and differences. They won't compare you to others or make you feel inferior. Furthermore, they don't use peer pressure to make you do things you don't want to do.

They Love to Exploit You

A toxic friend is there during fair weather – when they need something or when everything's okay but gone the minute you're in a storm or a struggle.

For this type of friend, you're their problem-vent. Somehow, when they are done, this friend asks you about your situation and then quickly changes the conversation's focus back to themselves again.

Remember that a true friend empathizes with your concerns under all circumstances, and they aren't just takers; they also give.

They Want to Remake You

True friends accept you for who you are since they understand that every individual has a different personality. They don't try to change you unless you ask their guidance to change something in yourself. Instead of being dominant and telling you outright about what you should do, they'll wait for you to ask them their opinion.

For example, if you want to be better at socializing with other people or want to meet new peers, they suggest that you come with them, so they can introduce you to some of their good peers you can find comfortable. On the other hand, toxic friends do exactly the opposite.

THE IMPACT OF
TOXIC FRIENDSHIP ON TEENS

Spending your time in a toxic friendship as well as any other toxic relationship creates a significant, adverse impact on your whole well-being as it can affect both your emotional and physical health.

Take time to observe yourself and look for any of these signs after spending time with any of your friends. In case you see these signs, think about re-evaluating that friendship.

Social Isolation

A natural positive result of true friendships is that when you spend time with them, your sense of connection increases.

On the contrary, toxic friends leave you with the sense of being ignored. When you try to reach out and make plans with them, you're left out of the events, and your messages are most likely unanswered unless you can provide them with something they need.

You may feel that they don't seem like they want to hang out with you. The 'friendship' that they offer doesn't feel fulfilling nor like friendship at all.

More Stress

When you are loaded with stress, strong friendships reduce it (Wojciechowski, 2021). However, they can't always make you feel at your best. If not better, visiting your friends can improve your mood at least.

However, instead of relieving stress, toxic friends add to your stress as they can do or say something that will upset you while you're together.

Also, even if you're away from them, you could tend to think back on your times with them, and remembering it could make you irritable, tense, or way too awful.

The Absence of Support

With true friends, you'll get support when you need it the most though there are times that you don't get tangible support from them. Not only that, true friends listen and empathize. When they feel that you are in pain or distress, they will try their best to make you feel validated.

This is not so with toxic friends, as you will never receive support nor compassion from them. More than likely, they'll just ignore your problems, messages, or requests for help. This will only make you feel minimized and totally ignored. Thus, don't expect them to be there for you when you need them to be there.

Diminished Self-Confidence

It's a norm for toxic friends to put you down whenever you're together. But when that continuous, habitual way of putting you down becomes a part of your daily routine, it will eventually find its way into your subconscious until you start believing and accepting it as your personality. Eventually, you will end up doubting your own strengths and capabilities, and your self-confidence will be diminished.

Taking the Blame

Even when these friends become mean to you, you begin to think that you are wrong and that you deserve what they are doing to you. This may be an outcome of their manipulation. But still, you try to make up for them by making yourself available and too accommodating whenever they need you or something from you. Worse, you might even feel grateful that they keep your company since you have so many flaws that they have pointed out.

Off-Balanced and Confounded

Manipulation is a tactic often used by toxic people to get what they want or need (Langslet, 2020). It often gives you the impression that something is not right, and you can't pinpoint what that is.

With them, you can never know if you are saying or doing the right thing. They react or overreact in ways that unbalance and confound you, so you tend to use extreme caution whenever you are with them. They openly mock you or dig subtly at you, which leaves you uncertain if they mean what they say. They can shout at you or laugh their heads off at any situation which can make you uneasy. Being in such situations could affect other parts of your life, making you easily upset or jumpy.

Negatively Affects Other Relationships

Like poison, toxic friendships can also gradually contaminate your other close relationships. How? When you begin to lose your self-confidence, you probably think of yourself as good-for-nothing and as a result, avoid people. You might also find trusting others difficult for you. Then, isolate yourself and stop looking for other friends who are supportive and will truly care for you.

HEALTHY SOLUTIONS FOR TEENS

If you or your teen have found yourselves in a poisonous friendship, you have these options.

Offer Your Friend a Second Chance

Talk to Your Friend. It is possible that they don't realize that their behavior is unpleasant. It could be a good choice if you value that friendship so much that you want to save it.

Move On With Your Life

End the Friendship. Just leave and save yourself before your energy is drained.

RIGHTS WAYS TO CHOOSING RIGHT FRIENDS

Choosing the right kinds of friends is critical to your child's success. Teaching them how is a way to safeguard their future. Here are ways for your child to pick the right set of friends.

Associate Yourself With Productive People

Who wouldn't want to take their life, career, or business to the next level? To be able to do this, associate with people who belong to that group. It's easy to reason with yourself that you feel most comfortable with those like you in so many ways, but being with the 'higher group' can help to expand your mindset or vision for greater possibilities. They can also expose you to new information, a higher level of living, and more extraordinary things. When you learn to value these friendships, you can find advancement too.

Find People With Similar Values and Aspirations

Every person's character differs from another but when it comes to your core friends, choose those who have the same goals, values, and aspirations as you. It will keep you from getting into compromises and being influenced negatively by those who don't share the same standards and values as you. On the other hand, like-minded friends who uphold similar values can help you be accountable to yourself and them.

Try to Befriend People Who Share Similar Goals

When you have friends with similar goals, you can push one another. As partners with the same purpose, you can work on, encourage, and reach your goals together.

Find Friends Who are Compatible With You

All persons have strengths and weaknesses, but being with the right friends could be very beneficial, especially when they have the skills, talents, or abilities you lack.

Let's say you are not good at organizing things. Ask the help of a friend who has the organization skill.

If you find your friend having difficulty in something you are an expert in, offer assistance. This way, you can both be successful as you utilize each other's best assets.

Stick With Friends Who Inspire and Motivate You

Do you want to be with somebody down or hostile all the time? Typically, any person under normal circumstances wants to be around people who are positive and uplifting. Observe your friends to determine if they are on the positive or negative side. Observe your conversations and how they sounds. You will know your friends are great "purpose partners" if they are always ready to listen to you and help you be positive-minded regardless of the situation.

Befriend People with Similar Interests

You will enjoy the company of people who have the same interests as you. It could be good music, sports, or performing arts – as long as you enjoy hanging out and doing things together, you will establish stronger bonds with each other. Also, you will have someone to go with you as you visit new places and enjoy new experiences.

Befriend People Who Pursue Knowledge

It's great to have friends that embrace learning – you can learn, grow and advance through them. These friends will share information or suggest good books that will help you with your journey in life. Avid readers are fun to talk to, for they are great in conversations.

Find Friends Who Can Be Your Purpose Partner

Purpose partners are those you share your dreams and goals with and encourage you to achieve them. Let's say you tell that friend what you intend to do. That friend will help you stay accountable to move on towards that plan. Allow that friend to ask about your progress. You could do that to them, too.

Find Friends Who Would Love To See You Succeed

Whenever you reach a milestone, gain accomplishments, and make success stories in your journey, true friends will celebrate (not only tolerate) you. They are the first group of people, along with your family, to congratulate you and are genuinely happy when they see you succeed. Keep them close if you have such friends, for they can be rare.

Find Friends Who Strive for Achievement

You are the achiever type of a person if you are serious about your goals and success. Wasting time on frivolous pursuits and casually living life is not your game as you want to get things done fast-paced. So, if you think you are an achiever, consider people who also value achievements as you do.

Pursue a Give and Take Friendship

All healthy relationships are defined as a give-and-take relationship, and this is the same with friendship. If you want to have great friends, be one yourself. Treating people in a nice way is not only rewarding but can also be fulfilling as well.

If your friends fit the criteria above, you are not far from having long-term success and boosting the quality of your relationships. But if not, consider finding friends who do and establish healthy relationships.

As you help prepare your kids to achieve their future success, it is important that you keep track of people who are around them. Knowing that your teen goes with the right set of friends can put your mind at peace. Ensure that you provide them with the skills to identify the right ones and keep your distance from those who are toxic. Conversing with them on a regular basis helps you know who their friends are and if they are choosing the right ones.

Chapter 4

HOUSE RULES FOR TEENS

*a*s parents, we should not only focus on academic education. It is also important to discipline and control your teenage kids, as they are always subject to temptations.

WHY IS IT NECESSARY
TO HAVE HOUSE RULES?

Your home is a place for training. As parents, you must instill values and discipline in your kids as part of their training. Without training and discipline, they will find it hard to battle life's challenges and face the outside world.

Establishing house rules is a component of this training. House rules will serve as healthy boundaries, which will help develop your kids' values, behaviors, and principles (Kid'sHealth, n.d.). How one adheres to family rules determines how one can follow the rules in the community and the state they live in. House rules are the fundamental components of discipline. Here are the benefits that every child can reap by following house rules.

Teach Your Teen Life Skills

What parents tend to miss here is none other than the connection between rules and self-control. As children mature, their ability to resist impulsivity and temptation lessens, making it the parent's role to protect those children from themselves. Teens need to learn self-control by setting rules for themselves, which is done by having household rules.

If they refuse to obey household rules, there is no way for you and them to be happy. Children who fail to follow household rules will never be able to learn self-discipline. So even though it is uncomfortable to stand up to teens and assert household rules, by doing this, parents are doing their teens a considerable favor in the long run. Aside from self-control, household rules also provide scaffolding supporting teens as they build themselves up to become both respectable and responsible.

If you're not convinced about your kid's lack of self-control, observe their screen time. Without rules or restrictions, teens will spend up to nine hours a day holding their phones or personal computers. While it is still unclear how much screen time affects the body, we are still aware that it drastically cuts their sleeping time. So while teens lack the self-control to minimize their screen time, it's the parent's job to establish rules to prevent them from getting out of control.

Household rules also teach kids accountability. A teen who willingly obeys household rules has more perks given to them over time. For example, following their parents' limitations regarding their phone usage allows them more screen time in the long run. On the other hand, if teens choose to disobey the rule, the chances are that their phones might be taken away, in addition to having lesser screen time.

Even if it's relatively safe for teens to mess up sometimes, denying them the chance to practice being responsible is a big mistake. Those who don't have or obey household rules also won't pay attention to any other authority, regardless of whether they know that the existing rule is good or not. For example, if they can get away from breaking things inside their homes, it might become a habit to display vandalistic behavior outside their homes. And as we all know, the destruction of public property tends to have dire consequences such as jail time.

Additionally, household rules give teens a sense of boundaries or edges. They can also use it to justify themselves to their friends when they lack the courage to take a stand. They can say that their parents won't allow them to get out of the house whenever their friends invite them to a party that they do not feel like attending .

Tell Your Teen That Rules Give Structure

It is usual for your kids to test their limits. It can be frustrating indeed and test your patience as parents, but you must also know that this is how your teens can learn what is wrong and right. One way to help them learn and still maintain control is to create structure. Consistent rules and routines form the structure.

An example of this is if your children will not follow your direction, and you give a warning that they will be grounded if they don't follow the house rules. If your child insists on defying house rules as directed, then they will be grounded.

HOUSE RULES TO KEEP YOUR TEENAGERS IN LINE

As your children grow from being innocent and obedient to becoming teens that form their ideas and thoughts, you are responsible for leading them to the right path in life. Teenage years may be the most challenging period for any parent, where your parenting abilities are tested to the limits. At this stage in one's life, your child can learn values essential to success, such as integrity, discipline, and self-control.

To start that up, setting house rules are indeed necessary to ensure that they will become responsible adults in the future. However, it would be best to remember that these rules are not manipulating their developing freedom and creativity. But if you think your teen needs support in certain areas, don't think twice about being strict as you implement house rules.

Here we cover a set of helpful house rules to adopt and practice in your home.

A SET OF HOUSE RULES FOR CONTROL, DISCIPLINE, AND SAFETY

Here, you will find 21 house rules categorized into five types so you can easily understand and implement them with your children whatever age (younger kids, preteens, teenagers) they may be. These house rules will provide your kids great help and safety as they begin to get their hands on independence.

Rules for Safety

Newfound independence, when used without considering responsibility, could get your teen into trouble. Driving fast, going out at odd hours, meeting new people, or experimenting with drugs or alcohol could quickly get out of hand. But when you set limits, you can give them more freedom and be assured that they will be responsible for their actions.

Set Road Safety Rules

It's not surprising if you find your teen very enthusiastic about driving lessons. However, they should be at a permissible age (according to the law of your state) before allowing them to drive bikes or cars. Then, let them earn their license and establish road safety rules like the following:

➲ No speeding.
➲ No driving if you drink.
➲ No receiving phone calls or texts while they are driving.
➲ Wear a helmet or a seatbelt always.

In 2016, about 10,000 people died in the U.S. because of car crashes due to driving under the influence of alcohol (Mississippi Department of Transportation, n.d.). It is the primary reason why teens get involved in road accidents. Therefore, be strict about imposing this rule.

Check for Substance Abuse

Make it clear that your teenager is not to consume alcohol before they're of legal age. When they come to that age, discuss with them the adverse effects of excessive alcohol consumption.

You may not always be there to completely stop your teen from drinking alcohol altogether, but you can do something by setting down rules that can limit them from consuming too much until they know how to control themselves.

Place rules like:

➲ Drinking alcohol until they black out is not allowed.
➲ No experimenting with drugs.
➲ There is a particular limit or number of times that they can enjoy drinking.

Time Limit is a Must

Some parents allow their teens to come home late at night but keep in mind that this is not good for their safety and health.

Set a reasonable time when they should be home (e.g., at 8 p.m., they should be home), and when they meet that deadline, you could make it a reward by allowing them to stay out late on special occasions.

Also, make your teens a fixed schedule for bedtime on school days and holidays. The point here is about discipline- make sure that they go to bed at a specific time daily. Don't forget to explain to your teen why you are doing this so that they will not rebel.

House Party Rules

➲ Teens might like to invite friends over to your house for a party. So, you will also need to set some limits and rules for this occasion. They shouldn't arrange for a party if you are not there to supervise it.

➲ They should ask for your permission first before they organize a party under your roof.

➲ If you permitted them, your child should be responsible in case any absurd events happen.

If your child is starting to put up arguments about the rules, be patient, explaining what profound implications will occur if they behave irresponsibly.

Seeking Permission is a Must

It is possible that you might find yourself in a rather difficult situation as you implement this rule to a strong-willed teenager who wants to make their own decisions and feels that they are already grown up.

At some point, they may be suitable to choose what they think is right for them. However, as a parent, you need to set some rules that will guide them to safety.

Under any of these circumstances, they must inform you beforehand.

- ➲ Whenever they have plans to go on an outing or travel with their friends.
- ➲ If they can't beat your curfew time or the time when they need to be at home, they should at least call you and tell you their whereabouts regardless of the reason they might have.
- ➲ If they plan to have an out-of-town trip, they should tell you in advance and provide you with the full details.

As you impose these rules, your teen might take these as restrictions. However, you should explain to them that these house rules are for their safety. Once they earn your trust in their judgment, you can finally leave that up to them.

Rules for Teaching Ethics and Morality

Your teen is at a stage where they try to distinguish which is right from wrong. But without proper guidance, they might get the wrong perception of what is truly good or bad. Therefore, presented below are house rules that deal with ethics and morality.

Respect Everyone

- ➲ Make respect a golden rule that your teenager should always observe.
- ➲ Always respect parents or guardians.
- ➲ Guests should be treated with respect, and they should always be polite with them.

Acknowledge and Respond

Though you shouldn't present this as a rule to your child, this can still help you have healthy conversations with your child. Help your child understand that they need to acknowledge and respond to you every time you talk to them, whether they agree or disagree with what you are saying. When you do this, you will have a healthy relationship to understand each other's point of view.

87

No Physical and Verbal Abuse

These are obvious signs of disrespect. Point out to them that if they abuse someone physically or verbally (e.g., pinching, screaming, kicking, yelling at somebody, gossiping, name-calling, bullying), they disrespect them.

Remind them to be grateful and polite by saying 'please' and 'thank you' appropriately. Teach them to explain their points without sounding rude.

All people expect basic courtesies as part of etiquette, and parents are responsible for teaching their kids to treat others with respect. So, tell your teens to give respect to gain respect from others.

Honesty

Having integrity is vital, so teach your children to be honest and make it clear that lying is unacceptable. Your teens need to be honest with you- meaning that they should not hide the truth or omit details- all the time.

Encourage honesty always. Promises are kept and not meant to be broken.

If you want honesty to be developed in your child, make sure that you and your spouse are both excellent models for your teen. Honesty is a trait that is formed through observation.

Ask First to Borrow

Teach your child not to borrow or take anything from anyone unless they asked for the owner's permission first. Whoever that may be: a family member, neighbor, or friend- ask first. Tell them that if they get something without asking for it first, it could be mistaken as stealing, which is a crime.

Lastly, if they borrowed something, they have to return it in the same condition it was before borrowing.

No Knocking, Don't Enter

Teach your kids to knock always before they enter someone's bedroom. Before they enter the parents' or siblings' room, they should knock and wait for a response first. As for parents, they don't need to wait for a response before they enter their children's room after knocking. Also, peeping into a room is not allowed. No matter how close you are to your child, advocate privacy respect.

Rules for Building Healthy Habits

Rules are ideal yet practical tools that help children form healthy personal habits. These rules could help you build those healthy habits within your teen's personality.

Do Homework

It's common knowledge that if you want to secure good grades, go to school regularly and complete your homework in time. However, this tends to become an issue with teens as they get bored or spend a lot of time doing homework. But if you set some rules regarding it, homework issues can be resolved.

Rule examples:

➲ Complete homework first before you go out with your friends or watch TV.

➲ If a teen's lesson is complex or it requires your help, they should ask you.

➲ Teenagers should set their schedule for doing their homework.

Limit Gadget Use

Limit teen's use of gadgets by implementing rules to prevent them from getting addicted to them. Cell phones or computers may be necessary but should not be used excessively. Here are some things you could do to prevent your teen from gadget addiction.

- ➲ Let your child pay for their purchase if they want a cellphone.
- ➲ Phone usage should have a specific time limit.
- ➲ Don't use phones while at the dinner table.
- ➲ Disallow phone usage at certain hours of the night.
- ➲ Set standards and rules regarding online relationships and social media posts.

These things will encourage them to save money and earn the privilege of using the phone or computer.

Here are some rules for using a computer:

- ➲ Use the computer for only a limited time.
- ➲ Access to websites that are inappropriate for your teen's age is restricted.
- ➲ Permit them to use the laptop after they finished their homework only.

TV, Video Games, and Movie Rules

Impose rules regarding the following:

- ➲ When they can be allowed to watch TV, play video games, or go to a movie.

⮑ What kind of games, films, and channels are they allowed to access.

⮑ Until when (time limit) they could watch TV or play games every day.

Rules for Equipping Them With Life Skills

College life means that your teens will live independently, do things without your help, and find ways to solve their problems. Though parents would always prefer to keep their kids close, a time will come when you need to let them go. So you need to prepare them for the inevitable through the help of specific house rules that will equip them with the skills required to survive the world outside your home.

Do Assigned Household Chores

A general rule for a house should include doing household chores.

Assign and let your teen do a few simple household chores. Chores should be done on time, and no one should be exempted from doing that unless your teen is out of the house or sick.

Some chores that your teen could do are:

⮑ Cleaning the table after a meal.

⮑ Washing dishes.

⮑ Walking the dog.

⮑ Taking out the garbage.

⮑ Doing laundry on a particular day.

⮑ Keeping away their bags, clothes, and shoes as these shouldn't be left cluttering the house.

The idea here is to teach your child basic household management skills as they help you with the chores around the house. But you could also exempt them from doing chores sometimes (and not always), like when they have a lot of school work, exam periods, or extracurricular activities.

Enforce Cleanliness

Habit-forming of cleanliness should start not only during adolescence but even at the early stage of childhood. Teach your child to be clean through these rules:

⮑ Clean your room daily.

⮑ Make your bed after you wake up.

⮑ Used clothes are to be put in the laundry basket and not to be left lying on the floor.

- ⮑ Clean your bathroom and closet.
- ⮑ If they take something out of the fridge, they have to put it back after use unless it's empty.

If your child learns to value and develop cleanliness through these rules, it won't be hard for them to get along with somebody (e.g., roommate, friend, special someone, or spouse) if they have to share space with them.

Responsibility: Be Accountable

Take time to discuss with your teen the importance of making decisions and their corresponding consequences. Ask them if they are ready for that.

You need to explain to your teen that they should be accountable for every action they make and accept all the consequences that come with it. Complaining, whining, pouting, arguing, and crying can't change their situation once they already made decisions and acted them out.

Resolving into manipulation tactics to escape consequences such as making others feel bad, screaming, blaming others for something they did, and crying is not a good trait.

Moreover, it would be best to clarify that you are there to support them but cleaning the mess is their responsibility and not yours.

Rules for a Healthy Social Life

It's typical for teens to be active in their social life. That's why you'll notice that they like to hang out with their friends most of the time. It's also the age where they will start dating. It's up to you as the parent whether you'll allow them to socialize more or not. At least, set limitations until they act with self-discipline.

Date Rules

Do you want your teen to hide their relationship with the opposite sex? Give them some freedom to socialize with the other sex but set the boundaries. Enlighten them about infatuation and love, harmless flirting, and rules about mingling with the opposite gender. Discuss your concern about issues on safety (especially for daughters) like date drugs and date rape.

Dating rules that need to be established are:
- Dating is allowed if they have reached the appropriate age (let's say, at 16).
- Whenever they go out on a date, they should be back before your set curfew.

➦ They should inform you where they will go on the date.

➦ Physical contact (holding hands, kissing, and sex) is not allowed until they are at the right age.

You might have teens that will disagree with these rules but help them understand that as an adult, you have already been in their place, so you know more than they know. Please encourage them to stick with the rules.

Friendship Rules

You can't choose your teen's friends for them, but you can influence their choice by choosing good friends. Aside from that, you can also limit the hang-out time of your teen with their friends but try not to sound too controlling.

The pointers listed below are some things to consider when it comes to your teen's friends:

➦ Observe the persons who they spend time with.

➦ They must introduce their friends to you.

➦ Keep an eye on everything that your teen does while they are with their peers.

⮑ Teach them how to handle friend break-ups and bullying.

Prevent Unhealthy Emotional Expression

The teenage stage is when your kid becomes vulnerable to emotions, so they need your guidance on how they can deal with their overwhelming feelings. Your teen needs to regulate their emotions- meaning they express what they feel in a healthy way, not suppressing nor hiding those feelings and releasing them without aggression or violence.

RULES TO COVER EMOTIONAL SITUATIONS

Rules that will help them handle anger, fear, and jealousy.

⮑ Take a five-minute break if they are angry, and then talk about it afterward.

⮑ Make it clear that screaming, shouting, hurling abuses, throwing things, or any actions that can hurt somebody is unacceptable.

⮑ If you see your teen out of control, give them a break and be firm when you tell them that you will only hear them out once they calmed down.

⮑ Explain to your teen that when they go through negative emotions like anger or jealousy, it is essential that they express those emotions in a good way- not by harming others, not themselves either.

Encourage Open Conversation Through Listening

Encourage your teen to open up if something bothers them. Observing this significant family rule will yield a healthy parent-child relationship.

When your kids talk to you:

- ➲ Make them feel comfortable as they talk to you.
- ➲ Be a friend that listens without being judgmental to have honest, effective communication.
- ➲ Don't interrupt them while they speak, and wait for your turn to speak.
- ➲ Listen to your teens with an open mind. Avoid judging or determining whether they are guilty or not if you haven't heard them out yet.

As you show this kind of communication to your teen, you also teach them to communicate with others without offending the other party- a skill to be developed to garner success in relationships.

Parents set the rules, and teens should follow them. But it is for your teens to decide if they will follow the rules or not. Teach them why they need to follow these rules and help them understand how important rules are.

ENFORCING HOUSEHOLD RULES FOR REBELLIOUS TEENS

Applying rules of any sort to teens not used to having such will not become a linear process. In other words, parents should expect pushbacks or defiance of some kind whenever a particular rule is applied, and they do not like it. During this time, parents should be firm and serious while implementing such practices. You can also have a heart-to-heart talk with your teen if you want their cooperation. Acknowledge that you have made mistakes before, kindly explaining why household rules are essential in a way that they can understand. Teens will always appreciate an honest answer, so make sure to stay honest as much as possible.

Chapter 5

YOUR TEEN, SOCIAL MEDIA, AND INTERNET USE

*S*ocial media nowadays has become a part of almost every aspect of life, especially those who belong to the Social Media Natives or

Generation Z. Gen Z people belong in the group 7-22 and were born after 1997 ("Revised Guidelines Redefine Birth Years and Classifications for Gen X, Millennials, and Generation Z," 2019).

Social Media has significantly affected the lives of everyone, even though some have preferred to ignore it and continue their daily lives. However, people are engaging actively in social media platforms, from teenagers to grandparents. But the real question is: Is social media worth using by teenagers for engagement with all its pros and cons? But before you answer that, let's look at social media as a whole, mainly the positives and negatives of social media in youth.

TEENAGERS AND SOCIAL MEDIA

When we say social media, social media platforms such as Facebook, YouTube, Instagram, Twitter, Snapchat, etc., instantly come to mind. Such platforms have paved the way as a significant addition to the life of teenagers who use those said mediums.

Though Facebook may have gravely embedded its influence in the millennial generation, Gen Z teens are more active in using Instagram, YouTube, and

Snapchat than Facebook. But this doesn't guarantee that they don't have Facebook profiles as well.

In recent years, businesses and brands have heavily invested in social media to tap this ever-increasing market audience. It may be due to the fact that, according to statistics, 72% of the teenagers who see products on Twitter or Instagram make purchases.

Aside from these, teenagers also use social media for the following purposes:

- ➲ Making new friends.
- ➲ Keeping in touch with friends.
- ➲ Shopping online.
- ➲ Keeping up to date with trending events.
- ➲ News and information.

But because teens increased their social media engagement, this has instigated mixed, contradicting views and opinions. Let's proceed to the pros and cons of teens utilizing social media.

PROS OF SOCIAL MEDIA

Though there are many apparent benefits of social media usage, let's look at the top three pros of social media.

Up To Date Knowledge About News and Information

You can quickly notice that teens nowadays are more knowledgeable about the latest global developments than anybody else in the family. It means that news and information break out faster on social media than traditional media. The longer they stay tuned on these platforms, the more they know global happenings and issues that affect the globe. Examples of such problems added to their knowledge base are global warming, sexual harassment, terrorism, etc.

Being Independent in Conducting Studies and Research

Giving teens free access to social media and the internet can provide aid to study-related research that they conduct online. You can easily create case studies, tutorial submissions, and presentations with the information acquired from social media. It may mean relying on parents, tutors, or relatives for help will eventually subside as it will give way for teens to become confident and independent in their abilities.

Furthermore, informative and educational brands also venture to help students expand their businesses through social media platforms.

Developing and Increasing Self-Respect and Self-Esteem

Teens worldwide find help dealing with many issues that affect them from communities and pages on social media. These issues include drug abuse, sexual harassment, depression, and disabilities.

There are times that teens could have a tough time opening up sensitive issues to you. Still, with the help of social media pages, they are offered a ready ear for listening to the problems they are in, and in most cases, they seek active help to address those issues after discussion. Thus, communities serve as not only support groups for your teens but could also be their second families.

CONS OF SOCIAL MEDIA

Here are the three major disadvantages of social media for your teen:

Cyberbullying

Cyberbullying is happening online via social media and is considered one of the biggest hazards to your teen. Trolling, in particular, has become a full-time menace that makes teens its worst-hit target.

Because of cyberbullying, many teenagers are reported to have sought help from therapists due to morphed photos, stalking, nasty comments, and a wide range of unhealthy practices.

Losing Touch with Reality and Obesity

When your teen spends more time cooped in front of smartphones or any gadget online, they tend to forget the offline world and enjoy life with the internet. Recreational activities such as playing outdoors, swimming, and hiking are overlooked as your teens isolate themselves from reality. These scenarios show us increasingly alarming trends that produce empty parks, sports centers, and facilities.

Because of lack of physical exercise, teen obesity rates surge upwards and reach endemic proportions in developed countries like America and others. Obesity now becomes an issue for your teen due to lack of physical exercise.

Stress and Pressure

Has your teen recently asked you to buy something you think is unnecessary and post it on their social media account? If yes, this might be because teenagers feel pressured and stressed whenever they feel disconnected from the social media world.

You might be unaware of it, but social media is a pretentious world with its own rules. The only way your teen feels that they could be accepted or fit in that world is to post life events regularly. Many other teenagers also think that posting online is their way to stay relevant in the social media world.

However, the pressure of staying relevant on social media groups leads to depression, unmitigated trauma, and loss of connection with parents.

RED FLAGS

We all know that life is genuinely challenging, especially with the pandemic- which resulted in our children spending much, much more time online than when they used it before. Unfortunately, that is only an understatement for what is truly happening to our children nowadays. Most counselors and educators say that even if digital use and technology can be productive, it would be foolish if parents ignore the red flags they see on their children. So take decisive steps if you see these red flags on your child:

Disengagement From Normal Activities. When your teen suddenly shows some changes in behavior such as not eating well and poor or lack of sleep, it is possibly a sign that something online is troubling your child.

Sudden Change in Academic Performance. Something could be distracting your child from their coursework.

Usage of Gadgets at Odd Hours. Your child might be communicating with strangers that have shady characters if you see them using gadgets early in the morning or late at night. You must be alert to watch over your teens lest they will fall victim to unscrupulous characters.

Disengagement From Old Friends. If your child suddenly stops hanging out with old friends, it could be that they are feeling that their friends would be judgmental of what they are doing online.

Sudden Increase of Expenditures. They could be investing in shady businesses or purchasing too many products online.

WHAT'S WRONG
WITH SOCIAL MEDIA?

Kids and teens are constantly engaging in social media. Though social media has many good things to offer, there are also plenty of risks that your teens must be aware of and should avoid. An example is when teens make wrong choices on posting something to their social media site, resulting in problems. So, it's crucial to open up and guide them in using social media wisely.

It's good when your kids get or learn these things from social media:

- ➲ Stay connected with their family and friends.
- ➲ Their creativity is enhanced by sharing ideas, art, and music.
- ➲ Get involved or volunteering for a charity, campaign, or nonprofit organization.
- ➲ They are having meetings and interactions with people who share the same interests.
- ➲ They communicate with fellow students and educators.

On the other side, you can also find cyberbullying and questionable activities on social media sites.

Without extra concern about privacy, your teens could share more information about themselves online than they should be sharing.

These are examples of what most teens share online that make them susceptible or easy prey for online predators that could harm them:

- ➲ Share their real identity (name) and post their photos on their online profile.
- ➲ Reveal their interests and birthdate.
- ➲ Post their location, including their school's name and the place where they reside.

As a result of not being careful about their private information, many teens had experienced the following situations:

- ➲ A stranger has contacted them in a way that made them feel uncomfortable or scared.
- ➲ To get access to websites, they lied about their age.
- ➲ They received inappropriate online advertising with regards to their age.

If parents don't monitor their kid's online activities, it would be easy for their kids to fall prey to the hands of internet predators. So make sure that you educate your kids about internet hazards so they are aware of the existence of these people online. However, that is not enough. You have to safeguard their devices as well.

CONCERNS AND CONSEQUENCES

Aside from online predators and cyberbullies, it's also possible that your teen could meet dangerous persons. Many apps automatically reveal the poster or user's location. Through these apps, it's easy for those dangerous people to have an encounter with your teen.

There are also issues about posted photos, comments, and videos that can't be permanently deleted from the internet. Although your teen thinks that what they posted is already deleted, it is still recorded on the internet.

Inappropriate posts like photos that could tarnish or damage reputations and mean-spirited texts meant as jokes could cause too much hurt or be taken as a threat and could still cause problems even after several years have passed. For example, a college admissions officer or a potential employer conducts a background check and finds such photos of your teen across the internet.

Moreover, teens could feel depressed or inadequate about themselves when they see posts of their "friends" having fun. It could be because it seems to them that they don't measure up with their group. So, you see, spending too much time on social media could make them feel down and lead to depression.

WHAT PARENTS CAN DO

Parents are not exempt from knowing what their teens are up to when they are involved in social media. But then, if you monitor their activity without their knowledge and they find out, it could damage their trust in you and alienate them from you. So, the best way to do this without being disrespectful to your kids' privacy is to clarify with them that you want to stay involved with them to ensure that they are safe and that you still respect their privacy.

Make sure that your kids know and do these necessary things:

Be Nice at All Times

Make it clear that being mean is not right and that you expect them to be respectful, and that they shouldn't make embarrassing or hurtful posts. If they receive bullying or harassing messages, tell them to confide it in you and never keep it to themselves.

Always Think Twice Before You Click "Enter"

Remind them that people could use what they posted against them. For instance, you could give robbers a chance to rob your house if the world knows you're off for vacation and you have your home address on easy access over the internet.

Furthermore, remind your teen not to post specific locations of events like parties and their phone numbers.

Practice the What-Would-Grandma-Say Rule

Let your teen ask themselves what they wouldn't want grandma, college admission officers, teachers, and future bosses to see. Then, teach them not to share those things on social media.

Check Their Privacy Settings With Them

Make sure your teen understands what privacy settings are for and how important are they as you both go through your teen's privacy settings on each account. Explain why passwords are important and why they shouldn't share passwords with anyone, including boyfriend, girlfriend, and best friend. Remind them that passwords protect them against identity theft and other people who could use their information to gain/ evil intentions.

Don't Befriend and Entertain Strangers

Tell them not to entertain strangers, especially online, to ensure their safety.

Make a Contract or Agreement

Try making a written agreement for social media use with your kids. Your teens should sign in the understanding of:

- ➲ Protecting their privacy,
- ➲ Considering their reputation,
- ➲ Avoid giving out personal information,
- ➲ Not to use technology to hurt others through gossip or bullying.

As for your part of the agreement:

➲ Agree to respect the privacy of your teen.

➲ You can also participate in social media and have them as one of your friends so you can monitor their online activities. However, avoid posting negative comments that would embarrass your teen.

If your teen breaches the agreement, the consequences would be to keep them grounded online by limiting their social media use.

Computers, laptops, and smartphones are not to be used in bedrooms and are kept in the house's common areas. There are also rules on technology that should be set (e.g., no gadgets or devices at the dining table).

Lastly, be a good model. When you exemplify, good virtual behavior will inspire your teens and help them learn how to use social media safely.

THREE SOCIAL MEDIA SCAMS TO WARN KIDS ABOUT

Is your child engaging in social media? It's not surprising to know that your teen is indulging in it since this is the modern way of social interaction.

Indeed, you may find social media beneficial in numerous ways, but it could still be hazardous for teens and even for some adults. However, tech-savvy teens are still most likely not that knowledgeable and haven't developed the ability to identify scams.

In that case, your teen would be very susceptible to becoming prey to online fraudsters who won't think twice about attacking your unsuspecting youth.

But then, you can prevent these scams from happening to your teen that would later become a devastating catastrophe by having an early discussion with them about online safety. Listed below are three scams your teen must be aware of lest they become a target.

Phony Contests

These are fake contests and surveys that seem to look legitimate but are designed and used by fraudsters to gather personal information that they sell.

Here, your teen would be answering questions about their mother's maiden name, a pet's name, or a favorite book - answers to which they used these answers for authentication purposes. They are using personal details to hack personal accounts.

Instascam

People named this scam after a popular photo-sharing platform - Instagram. As the name implies, an instascammer's modus operandi is to make quick money using the comment section of your photos. Because instascammers are using fake profiles of celebrities and influencers, kids may believe these people are legit.

Catphishing

This is considered one of the scariest scams that can target teens. Here, the fraudster pretends to be someone else and befriends the target intending to take personal information, money, or anything that seems to be valuable for them. Usually, they impersonate people who need help and live abroad or a youth who is looking for friends. They also request to chat with their target through a messaging service or via email.

PROTECTING YOUR TEEN FROM SCAM

Indeed, you can't be with your child 24/7, but there are things that you can do to protect them.

Keep in mind that if there are still full-grown adults who easily fall prey to various online scams, it won't be unusual for kids to become victims. You as a parent might not be able to monitor your child's internet activity every hour of the day, so you should take steps to protect them. Always remind them to refrain from talking to strangers, both online and offline. Additionally, warn them about following various 'Celebrity Profiles,' usually made by someone with either unknown or questionable identity.

Be open and discuss these scams with your child. It is common knowledge that social media accounts require users to be of legal age (18 years old and above), but teens can bypass this requirement by lying about their age. If this is the case with your child, you can either close that account or check that their account's privacy settings are set appropriately.

Remind them that if they don't know the person, they should not accept the friend request, and they should be aware of celebrity profiles that are mostly not legit, for they don't see the person running the profile.

Continuously monitor your teen's social media accounts. Turn off the geolocation setting and uninstall those apps that have access to your teen's data.

To enhance your kid's protection level, remind them never to give the following details to strangers:

- ➲ Account numbers.
- ➲ Social Security numbers.
- ➲ Any personal information.

If you believe that your child was victimized by a social media scam, start by immediately reporting to the local police.

WHAT PARENTS MUST KNOW ABOUT SEXTING

Sexting or sex texting refers to receiving or sending messages, images, or videos on the phone via the internet that suggest sex explicitly or implicitly. It includes:

- ➲ Text messages that refer to sex acts or that propose sex.
- ➲ Nearly or completely nude selfies or photos.

➲ Videos that show sex acts, nudity, or simulated sex.

WHY DO TEENS INDULGE IN SEXTING

Teens, provided with gadgets, could easily access the internet, wherein they could share private videos or photos of themselves even without the knowledge or consent of their parents.

When you ask teens why they engage in sex texting, you will get a range of answers:

For girls: They indulge in sexting as a way of getting attention, a joke, peer pressure, or because guys pressure them.

For guys: Because of peer pressure sometimes.

For some:

➲ Sexting is almost a normal behavior.

➲ It seems cool.

➲ It is a way to flirt.

➲ It is becoming popular .

Moreover, teens somewhat get support and approval for sexting when they see lewd pictures or videos of celebrities that go mainstream. These celebs often reap greater fame and earn reality TV shows instead of being humiliated and their careers ruined.

CONSEQUENCES OF SEXTING

Problems could indeed arise because of improper behavior such as sexting, so it's important to make your teen understand its consequences. Here are just some examples of those consequences:

➲ All sent items on the internet, such as pictures, videos, and messages, never genuinely go anonymous or private. It can take only a few seconds for the entire humanity to see what you sent across the internet.

➲ Whatever you post or transmit (image, text, or video) is already out of your control, even if it was only meant for one person. Even if you think it's deleted, it could still exist on the internet, and there's still a chance that others might see it.

➲ You could be embarrassed, humiliated, and publicly ridiculed if a compromising image is seen publicly or, by the least, sent to other people.

➲ Damaged self-image could lead to mental health issues or depression.

➲ Legal consequences may occur. Some states may press felony charges or have you registered as a sex offender because of texting explicit photos.

Risky online behaviors could still affect your future as a college applicant or a job seeker. Colleges and employers sift candidates by looking at their online profiles for signs of maturity or warning signs about lousy judgment.

ESTABLISHING RULES AND PRACTICES FOR ONLINE SAFETY

There are plenty of things that you could do as a parent to prevent and ensure that your teen is kept away from porn, talking to online strangers, and posting provocative pictures of themselves on social media. It would indeed be wonderful to know and implement all safety measures in the online world.

There is no way you can guarantee that your youngster won't do anything that could be a potential cyberspace danger. But there are ways in which you could diminish the probability of your child acquiring behaviors that will offshoot internet behavioral issues.

But first, you should aim to shape your family into a technology-reduced one. You could reach this goal by encouraging your children to put less emphasis on the digital world and more on the real world. This way, they can value and put energy into their real lives. It will also affect healthy web usage; they would only use it to learn about the world (as a necessity basis) or reach out to other people and not just search for the next adventure by constantly trolling in the cyber world.

Establish family rules and practices on online safety measures. Here are ten steps:

Learn the Modern Technology

Get familiar with all technology, apps, and websites that they use. If your youngster uses technology (of course they are!), so should you- even if it is only for just getting familiar with that technology or for setting up parental control features. Meaning to say, if they have laptops or an Xbox, you must learn how to use them and be comfortable with them. There is an app called Guide for Parents to learn about the latest apps and how they function. You could also search videos on YouTube on how to use parental control features.

Aside from that, explore how teens use social media sites and about other online behaviors. Facebook is not the only place where to find them.

Secure Privacy Settings

Look for and use the parental and privacy settings on all of your youngsters' devices such as phones, tablets, game consoles, laptops, and desktops. Though teens can bypass these settings (if they know how), others can be slowed down or hindered by them, and younger kids can't get around them.

Make Use of Monitoring Tools

Although you are very confident that your teen already knows the boundaries you've set for internet use, it's still necessary that you install software monitoring apps or programs.

Check their devices continually and if you see that they got around that software. If so, reinstall it.

Be open to your teen about your monitoring. There's a good chance that your child would feel that you invade their privacy if they find out that you do it secretly, and that could affect your relationship with them.

Teach Them the Importance of Building Good Online Reputation

Tell your kids how significant their online reputation is. Remind them that whatever they post online, including videos, comments, favorites, and likes- all of these are made permanent on the internet.

They can start creating a positive online reputation through LinkedIn while keeping all their other social media profiles off-limits to the public. Most social media users keep their profiles public on Instagram and Twitter for situations like college admission committees doing online background checks on their applicants.

So, encourage your teen to avoid posting wild or sexy photos of themselves as their profile photos to protect their online reputation.

Set Limitations on the Use of Technology

Set up schedules (when you allow or disallow technology use) to limit screen time and technology use. You can also implement a tech curfew. For example, no internet after 8 p.m. or ban phone and tablet use from 5-7 p.m. Then, allow your teen a 30-minute break to respond to texts, messages, and emails until you have all devices off at 7:30.

If you decide to implement tech curfews, parental control software could also be helpful tools to enforce tech curfews. You can track your teen's time spent on games, Netflix, and Facebook. You can also follow up and tell your youngsters to monitor time if they use the computer for homework activities or recreational activities for those who use particular apps like Microsoft Word or Excel for schoolwork.

Lastly, some teens may be staying up all night on their devices while you think they are already sleeping. To make sure they won't get past you, disable the wifi at night, or better yet, confiscate their phone before sleep.

Set Rules on the Availability of Internet on Devices

Make all internet devices available on Home Public Areas only. Teens may find their way to take a peek at porn. But, if you make all devices available for use in the living room or den only, that would give them a hard time to watch it for hours daily or even to chat with harmful online strangers like pedophiles.

It's a good idea to disallow the use of phones, tablets, and laptops in bathrooms and bedrooms. Provide an area or a place where you could keep or lock away (only if needed). Let your teen have a clear idea that:

All devices belong to you. You are only allowing them to use it as long as they use it responsibly.

These devices are not their private property, so it is off-limits in private rooms.

Make Them Accountable for Their Online Behavior

Teach your child to become accountable for their online behavior by making them sign a contract on technology behavior which includes an agreement to digital behavior rules that you set and their corresponding consequences if they broke the deal.

Make them understand that whatever behavior they display in cyberspace is also shown in public or real life.

So, if they don't want to show or do that before people they actually see, they shouldn't do it online.

Take note: Big kids tend to rationalize their mean behavior more than little kids who easily understand this concept.

Mentor Teens on the Responsible Use of Internet

Parents aim to teach their children to be independent in almost all areas, such as emotions, finances, chores, social bonds, etc., including their children's exposure to the digital world.

Who wouldn't want their children to be capable of taking care of themselves anyway?

If you try keeping your teens from using technology, it will work against them once they get exposed to the competitive world. Preventing them from acquiring knowledge on technology will make them ignorant of regulating their digital behavior once they are out of your care.

However, this is not applicable for kids under 14 who don't have the developmental ability to regulate their digital behavior. In short, they still need your help to monitor and block things as much as possible until the time they have earned your trust, and you loosen your cyber-hold on them gradually.

Respect Teen's Privacy

Respecting your teen's privacy never means you leave everything up to them and that you are not allowed to monitor their digital activities. It is more about you protecting them.

Privacy respect includes:

- ➲ Providing physical privacy such as knocking before you enter their bedroom.
- ➲ Allowing them access to sexual health websites (if you are filtering their web use, you may have to enable it manually).
- ➲ Providing books about the body or about sexuality to read on their own.
- ➲ Allowing them to have a private conversation over the phone or in-person with their friends.

Always clarify to them that they can also ask you questions about personal matters.

Spend Quality Offline Time with Your Teens

Provided you already carved out time when everyone is hands-off their devices, fill that available period with fun activities.

Make that fun time with you both creative and stress-free as much as possible so you can ensure that they would prefer and value face-to-face relationships and real-world living more than what they have online.

Finally, be a model yourself of what behavior or healthy attitudes you want your youngsters to have towards technology and the internet world.

HOW TO HELP YOUR TEEN AVOID SEXTING

Teens may find it hard to comprehend the long-term consequences of impulsive behaviors and how sharing everything now could risk their reputations in the future. But as the parent, it is your job to help them understand that such behaviors can lead to problematic life situations.

Start by telling your teen about how photos, emails, videos, and texts are permanent in digital space. A racy picture sent to a crush's phone could easily be shared with friends, posted online, get printed, and be ready

129

for distribution. If a boyfriend or girlfriend has a "potential-problem" image of your teen, it could be seen by another person or get distributed after a break-up and result in problems.

As you become more open about conversations on personal responsibilities and boundaries and how to resist peer pressure, you'll get it through them. Talk with them often and not just when you face the problem with them.

Don't forget to explain and remind them that once an image or message is sent, they can't take it back. The worst-case scenario could be: when others, who are not supposed to see it, see it, and it is spread to more and more people. To prevent this situation, teach your teen to follow the "WWGT" rule (What-Would-Grandma-Think Rule). If they think grandma shouldn't see it, they better not send it.

Lastly, make it clear that they will face the consequences if you catch them sexting. Set limitations to their device usage or confiscate it if it needs to be confiscated as the situation arises.

Chapter 6

DRUG AND ALCOHOL
EXPOSURE

*D*rugs and alcohol are now readily available, even to teenagers. As a parent, you have a significant influence on your kid's decision not to use drugs or alcohol, even as a solution to some challenges in life.

Most likely, grade school children have not tried any of these, which is why it is an excellent time to start talking about the dangers of drugs and alcohol and prepare your child for future opportunities.

Drug prevention starts with you – learning to talk with your kids about such complex topics. As a follow-up, schools may offer programs in support of what you began to teach your children.

Because you have a significant impact on your children's decision not to use drugs and alcohol, start talking to them and listen to what they say. You should help them make better choices, especially in choosing good friends.

There is no such thing as "it is too early" for teens to know and learn about illegal drugs and their bad effects on the human body. Some parents think that their kids are still too young, discussing serious matters like drugs and alcohol must come later when they are old enough. Because of this mindset, these parents fail to educate their children, allowing them to fall prey to bad influences. When this happens, it becomes too late for them.

It is up to the parents to nurture their children and determine what's best for them throughout their growth. Some parents never mention the word 'drugs' and make it seem like a boundary or uncharted territory. On the other hand, some parents educate their kids about this, instilling anti-drug messages as early as possible.

Some research shows that kids receiving the talk about drugs and strict house rules become less likely to experiment with those as they grow up. Experts suggest that parents can talk to their kids about this topic as early as eight years old. If you as a parent determine that this seems too early for them, they can learn it once they reach their teenage years. However, keep in mind that teens nowadays drink alcohol as early as fifteen years old, so it might be good to start creating awareness during those early years. That way, your parental talk with them will serve as prevention instead of a cure.

Sharing Information

Complete ignorance does not exist when it comes to topics about alcohol and drugs, so it would be good if you trade or share information with your kids regarding what they know about those. You might be confident that they are not trying those, but still, it doesn't mean that they are completely ignorant about it. After all, teens are curious beings and absorb knowledge as fast as a dry sponge absorbs water.

Do not forget to ask them what they know and if they saw someone trying or using drugs. As a parent, make it a two-way conversation to keep them engaged in whatever you tell them.

Warn Them About Peer Pressure

Teens are naturally social, so it is only natural for them to have a friend or two that they trust. Other teenagers are so popular that they even have a distinguished peer group or clique, especially if they have an outgoing personality. In other words, having friends or even a peer group is not wrong.

However, there are times wherein friends or peer groups exert pressure on their members just for them to stay united. This pressure can turn out badly, especially if they use this to persuade their members to do bad things like trying or using drugs. As a parent, it might be good to mention this to your kids. Make them realize that having friends and peer groups is a good thing as long as they don't tell or force them to do bad things. Otherwise, it would be much better for them to stay alone.

Staying Honest About Personal Experiences

No one is perfect. Even parents experienced a bad thing or two during their teenage years. So whenever you, as a parent, may have experienced substance abuse, you can tell your children about it. However, emphasize that they should not try them but instead learn a lesson from your experience. It can also be a good opportunity for you to form a bond with your children through your personal experience, so they can relate to your struggles as you grew up. However, keep in mind that there are events in your life that you need to keep to yourself.

Continue with the Education

It is not enough that you manage to teach your teens about the dangers of illegal substances. Your responsibility to them goes beyond that. Even when you are sure that your teens are not involved in drugs, it is still worth reminding them from time to time.

It is also helpful to provide additional information about the topic to make them think twice about trying them. Since mentioning substance abuse to your teen is a form of education, it is your responsibility to teach them about it constantly.

Set Rules and Clear Expectations

Informing your teenage kid about illegal substance abuse and its consequences is not enough. Ensure to establish and enforce rules about unlawful substance use, laying out the appropriate punishments loud and clear once they decide to break those rules. Teens that stay in homes with household rules against substance abuse tend to stay away from those. On the other hand, homes that do not enforce house rules against this tend to have children who are more likely to smoke, drink, or use drugs. Keep in mind that being upfront with these things will not make your children hate you. Instead, they may feel cared for and looked after, eventually making them do something that will make you proud.

Remember that parents are the most decisive influence that children may have, and there is no guarantee that your child won't use drugs or alcohol, but they are less likely to happen if you:

- ➲ Spend more time with your kids and build a better relationship with them,
- ➲ Promote awareness on the dangers of using drugs and alcohol,
- ➲ Provide guidance and clear rules,
- ➲ If you don't use them yourselves ,
- ➲ If you drink alcohol which is unavoidable in some cultures and conditions, do so in moderation.

8 USUAL REASONS WHY TEENS TRY ALCOHOL AND DRUGS

Nowadays, more and more teenagers try to abuse alcohol and drugs. Because of this, parents should be aware and stay vigilant when it comes to their teen's activities. Even though there is no single reason why teens do drugs and alcohol, there are issues that may influence the behavior behind substance abuse.

Listed below are some of them.

Other People

It is usual for teens to see many people consuming various substances nowadays, both inside and outside their homes. It could be in the form of their parents drinking alcohol whenever there's an occasion or party, or it could be a group of teenagers doing the same thing while partying in a disco or club. It could also be in the form of their friends urging them to drink alcohol just for fun or comradeship. When this happens, the possibility of them trying those will become high.

Popular Media

Television and social media can become a reason behind drug addiction in teens when left unchecked.

Movies and TV shows depicting drug or alcohol abuse as an incredible thing are bad influencers for teens. To prevent this, make sure that parents monitor their kid's television and internet activities as much as possible.

Escape and Self-Medication

When teens cannot find a healthy outlet for their frustrations or pent-up anger, they will likely resort to alcohol or drug abuse. Depending on the substance that they use, they might feel unusually happy or satisfied with themselves. Those challenging teenage years often cause depression and anxiety to our teens that so many of them can't resist when given something to make them feel better.

Substance abuse does not just refer to the usage of illegal drugs like marijuana or cocaine but also includes prescription medicine like stimulants or over-the-counter medications like cough syrups.

Boredom

Teenagers who cannot tolerate being alone or crave excitement are usually the first ones who resort to alcohol and drug use. Not only do these substances give them something to do; it also helps them feel better by 'filling' the void within themselves. It also gives them a way to instantly bond with like-minded teens or groups.

Rebellion

Depending on their personality, teens might resort to illegal substance use to show that they are defying their parent's authority. Angry teenagers usually resort to alcohol because it allows them to behave aggressively. On the other hand, teens with escapist or misunderstood personalities resort to drugs since it provides them a 'personal world' to live in. When paired with a rebellious nature, they might even include cigarette use to exert their independence and defy their parents.

Instant Gratification

Since alcohol and drugs make people feel terrific once they start taking effect, it might become an ideal way for teens to release their pent-up frustration or anger. It might also become an 'ideal' medicine for their sadness.

Lack of Confidence

Shy teenagers resort to alcohol and drugs for them to gain that much-needed courage and confidence. If you're a lousy dancer, consuming alcohol gives you enough mettle to man the dance floor. It may also give them enough courage to sing despite having a bad voice quality. Because of these qualities, alcohol and drugs become tried-and-tested medicine to loosen one's inhibitions or alleviate social anxiety. When this happens, teens trying those eventually become addicted.

Misinformation

The wrong information or the lack of it is the usual reason behind teens trying alcohol and drugs. It is typical for a friend who is an expert on these substances to introduce them to your son or daughter. These people usually claim that the risks behind these substances are minimal and that the information provided to them by the parent, school, and authorities is merely an exaggeration.

SIGNS THAT YOUR TEEN USES DRUGS

It is indeed frightening to think or imagine that your teen might be drinking, smoking, or abusing drugs. And to think that it is becoming more rampant nowadays adds up to our list of worries. In 2015, more than half of high school seniors in the US admitted to drinking alcohol, and almost forty percent of them even used marijuana.

Drug use during the teenage years can cause complications that will affect the rest of their lives. As a parent or guardian, it is necessary to understand the signs and the right actions to take whenever these signs show up. Here's how:

Changes to Normal Habits

The person's family themselves knows the definition of what is normal or not normal. So whenever you, as a parent, notice that there are changes to your teen's 'normal' behavior, do not simply brush it off. Chances of them doing drugs might manifest if you happen to observe two or more of these things:

- ➲ Increased cravings or appetite,
- ➲ Poorer or lower grades,
- ➲ School complaints about misbehaviors,
- ➲ Changes in their group of friends,
- ➲ Lack of appetite sometimes.

Changes in Physical Appearance

Physical changes may vary depending on the drug being abused, so it might be somewhat hard to notice. However, there are still some noticeable changes to the teenage physique, such as:

- ➲ Unexplained wounds and puncture marks, or bruises around the arms,
- ➲ Bloodshot Eyes,
- ➲ Flushed Cheeks,
- ➲ Disheveled Appearance,
- ➲ Tremors or Uncontrollable Body Shakes,

➲ Dry Lips,

➲ Nosebleeds.

Secretive Behavior

It might be expected for teenagers with introverted personalities to stay aloof or secretive. However, if your child is extroverted but suddenly becomes secretive, it might be related to drug use. Other signs include:

➲ Avoiding Eye Contact,

➲ Staying inside rooms and locking doors,

➲ Missing or cutting classes, work, or extracurricular activities,

➲ Going out at night or vanishing from long periods without being noticed,

➲ Stealing.

Changes in the Home

It might not be possible for parents to find drugs and other illegal substances inside their homes, particularly their teen's rooms. However, parents should stay vigilant whenever they see unusual changes in the home environment, such as:

➲ Eye drops, cut aluminum foils, lighters, or matches,

- ➲ Containers or bottles that you cannot recognize,
- ➲ Missing drugs or alcohol inside the medicine cabinet,
- ➲ Used/Unused syringes and needles.

WHAT TO DO IF YOU SUSPECT YOUR TEEN USING DRUGS

Confront Your Teen

After compiling enough evidence, ask your teen about it directly instead of making accusations. Even if what you think is true, make sure to let them explain their situation. Doing this might be difficult, but you need to face it as a parent.

Have Your Teen Screened

On the other hand, if your teen still denies their drug use, you might as well let them undergo drug testing. Make sure that you know a doctor that can provide this service beforehand to avoid mishaps.

Set Boundaries

If your child has been caught doing drug or drinking alcohol, the first thing to do is change their lifestyle. If you permitted them to use your car before, ban them now. If they have a drivers license, take it away. Applying suitable punishment for their misbehavior will teach them that every wrongdoing has a consequence.

Get Help

In cases of teens addicted to drugs, your guidance as a parent will not be enough. They will likely need assistance to detoxify themselves from the substance, so doctors are required for this part. After your teens had undergone the detox process, a drug recovery program is essential for a full recovery. It will help your teen get back to everyday life and start a clean slate. Remember that despite your teen's strong willpower to change, still, they can't completely get away from addiction without intervention from outside.

Chapter 7

DATING AND ENTERING ROMANTIC RELATIONSHIPS

*a*s adults, we understand the joy and pain connected with romantic love and how it sometimes tips off the balance of our well-being. We know too well that extreme emotions experienced during chaotic teen years can be more damaging than advantageous.

As much as possible, parents want to shelter our children from situations that may give them lifetime scars. However, we also understand that we cannot protect them from these things all the time. On the other hand, what we can do is to help them be responsible for their relationship.

UNDERSTANDING TEENAGE RELATIONSHIPS

First things first— let's talk about how teenage relationships take place. Although, as adults, we had already gone through this phase once upon a time, only a few of us actually took time to reevaluate our teenage relationships.

Many have just moved on, dismissing those past relationships, well, as a thing in the past. They accepted it as part of life, a lesson to learn, and a beautiful memory— that's normal, and there's nothing wrong with that. But now, as a parent, this "thing in the past" should be reassessed and expressed for a child's understanding.

So, what are teenage relationships really about?

Romantic relationships are considered a crucial developmental milestone for any teenager. This type of relationship comes with physical, emotional, and social changes that happen during their adolescence. It is also closely connected to your child's growing interest in their own physical looks, image, privacy, and independence.

As we all know, romantic relationships can cause emotional ups and downs for your teenage child. This experience can, of course, affect the whole family. Thinking that your child would undergo this emotional turmoil can sometimes be challenging for parents.

However, you must understand that these feelings will help your child understand more about relationships. Romantic relationships also will help them to take part in, nurture, and develop intimate relationships.

THE START OF
TEENAGE RELATIONSHIPS

Every teen is unique, and every family has its own set of values regarding this issue. These age brackets will give you the general idea of when your child starts to reach their relationship milestones:

- ➲ **9 to 11 years of age:** Your child might begin to exhibit more independence from you and spend more time with friends.

- ➲ **12 to 14 years of age:** Your child might start to show more interest and spend more time in mixed-gender groups, increasing the probability of finding the object of their romantic interest. Those who belong in this age group also begin to engage in romantic relationships.

- ➲ **15 to 19 years of age:** Your child might find that their romantic relationship becomes the focal point of their social life. They also find that their friendships become more profound and stable at this point.

During their teen years, your children will spend a lot of time pondering and talking about being in a relationship— regardless of if it's platonic or romantic. However, these relationships might last only for a few weeks or months.

Conversely, you might be wondering why your child has never shown or talked about any interest in romance. It would be unfair to conclude that they're underdeveloped or something's wrong with them, especially when you're comparing them to your teenage self.

You have to understand that IT IS NORMAL for your child not to have any romantic interest until their late teens. There are several reasons for their disinterest in committing to a relationship. For one, it may be because they choose to focus and concentrate their efforts on academic studies, sports, hobbies, and other interests.

FIRST CRUSHES AND EARLY TEEN RELATIONSHIPS

We all had crushes during our younger days, right? It's just the same for our children. Before they begin having romantic relationships, they will experience having a crush on someone.

An *identity crush* happens when your child finds someone they admire, respect, and treat as a role model they want to follow and imitate. This type of crush often lasts longer because it is not focused on romantic feelings. Instead, it's all about using their crush as an ideal that helps shape their growth and development.

Being a parent, you need to respect the feelings of your child. However, you also need to get to know this "role model." If this role model exhibits behaviors or hobbies you believe won't be healthy or beneficial for your child, you need to talk about these things to them. On the contrary, your first impression of this person may not be good because of what you see on the surface. But you may discover what your child admires in them later on. Again, the key here is communication and constant monitoring to avoid severing your relationship with your child.

Meanwhile, a *romantic crush* is the development of romantic feelings. This admiration is formed when your child finds someone charismatic and attractive, who excites them, and whom they like to spend a lot of time with.

Sometimes, the object of their romantic crush is a person who's entirely their opposite but excites them anyway. For instance, your daughter has an outgoing, bubbly personality but has a crush on a quiet, mysterious boy who loves to read. Or your carefree son admires serious and practical girls.

Your child's romantic crushes can tell you a lot of things that they find attractive in people. While this type of crush may be short-lived because they get disillusioned over time, the intensity of your child's feelings is genuine. It is best to take these feelings seriously and not dismiss them or make fun of them.

When it comes to relationships, younger teens often hang out together in big groups or cliques. Among this group, they might meet up with someone special who can uniquely connect with them. Eventually, they will spend more time with the person alone.

Talking together about your child's desire to go out alone with this special someone can help you gauge whether your child is ready or not. These questions might help you with this endeavor:

- ➲ Does your child consider this special someone a boyfriend or girlfriend material?

- ➲ Why does your child feel that they should get involved in a romantic relationship with this person? Does your child want to commit to a relationship simply because their friends are in their respective relationships?

➲ How does your child feel about getting into a relationship? Do they think that being in one is just for fun? Or do they want it because they want to know their special someone better?

COMMUNICATING WITH AND GUIDING YOUR CHILD ABOUT TEENAGE RELATIONSHIPS

Guide your child with the basics of being in a relationship. For instance, does your child wants to be with someone younger or a bit older? It's worth mentioning that people of varying ages might have different sets of priorities in both relationships and life. Let's say that your sixteen-year-old daughter showed her interest in an eighteen-year-old graduating high school senior. You could point out that the other person would be busy and might not have the time for her. There's also the slight probability that he could be transferring to another state for college, making the relationship more challenging because of a long-distance relationship.

Talk with your child like their best friend. Do not use a condescending tone or be argumentative about your child's decisions. The more they perceive resistance from you, the more they could act rebelliously. Just like communication, respect is a two-way street. If you want them to respect what you say or decide on, then treat them with respect as well. This way, they will believe in their hearts, not only their minds, that you genuinely love and value them.

Always keep in mind that your family plays a significant role in how your child views relationships, particularly romantic relationships.

When you normalize conversations involving feelings, friendships, and family relationships, it will encourage your child to confidently share what happens to them inside or outside your home. Of course, this includes the friendships they formed, their crushes, or other relationships they have.

If your child understands how respectful and healthy relationships should be, they can easily relate this to romantic relationships. Your child will definitely feel more comfortable talking to you about their feelings as they begin to get romantically interested in others. These conversations can touch on crucial matters like treating people with kindness, respecting boundaries and limitations, and being compassionate despite the pain.

From a child's perspective, talking about sex and romantic relationships with their parents is somewhat awkward. You, yourself, might have grown up without opening these matters with your own parents because you felt that such issues were normally shared with closest friends only. Unfortunately, this is where mistakes usually start.

Just think about it— will sharing and trying to understand love problems with another greenhorn help render sound decisions? Would that be wise? Would that address the important questions you have in mind?

Now that you're already at the age where you have been through all those teenage woes, would you let your child obtain the "answers" to their problems from their peers?

Begin with having heart-to-heart conversations with your child about relationships and sex. Your child will want to know about the changes they are going through at this stage. On your part, you want to be their go-to person, their very first option whenever they feel discomfort over a particular issue they are going through. For this reason, you should show that you're a reliable parent and friend that will always be there for them whenever they feel worried, confused, or excited.

However, there is one thing you should never forget— you are a parent before a friend. Knowing this, you must establish family values and rules to guide all your decisions. Your child should know how they should behave as a precious member of the family. You will need to discuss behavior, ground rules, and the consequences of breaking these rules.

For instance, you would want to talk about how much time your child should spend with their girlfriend or boyfriend as opposed to how much time they should spend studying. You may also ask them to introduce this special someone to you and your spouse. You might also want to advise them how they should handle a situation wherein they feel threatened or unsafe.

Let them understand that while they may have friends with whom they could share their love woes, you are always there when they need a backup. Hence, they must keep the lines of communication open.

Dating and Entering Romantic Relationships

Some conversations associated with romantic relationships can be mentally and emotionally draining for both you and your child, regardless of your closeness. However, these discussions are crucial, especially when you believe that your child is not ready for a relationship.

MANAGING DIFFICULT TOPICS

Sex, for instance, is one of the most controversial topics you will have to tackle. It covers different areas that either you or your child might find embarrassing, distressing, and controversial. It could also be a topic that can trigger conflict or argument between both of you. Aside from sex, the issues that most families find difficult to discuss are:

- ➲ Secrets, Alcohol, smoking, and drugs,
- ➲ Academic difficulties and challenges,
- ➲ Work and money,
- ➲ Masturbation,
- ➲ Self-inflicted harm,
- ➲ Sexual orientation.

It's pretty normal to talk about these things discomfiting, but preparing your child about these life aspects should be prioritized.

So, how do you manage difficult conversations?

It would be best to ponder on these topics even before your child asks. If you put together a few takeaways about sex and teenage relationships, you will not be caught off guard and answer gibberish when your child asks questions like, "Mom, does it hurt the first time?" "How can I tell someone that I like them?" or "What is a wet dream?"

Here are five important key points that will help you handle challenging dialogues with your teenager:

➲ **Stay calm and be honest.** You don't need to hide the surprise, but reassure your child that you want to discuss the matter further. This way, you encourage them to talk about anything with you. Tell them that you appreciate how they turn to you for advice and answers.

➲ **Listen actively.** Teens quickly lose trust when they feel unheard or judged, so you need to give them a chance to talk through what's happening to them. Understand that, sometimes, they just need someone to hear them out without that someone trying to fix things for them.

➲ **Avoid patronizing your child all the time.**
Because we live busy lives, we find it more
straightforward to tell our children what to do
than spend time discussing issues with them.
However, this attitude alienates them from us.
Let your child know how you understand the
situation instead of forcing them to do what
you WANT because you BELIEVE that your
way is the right way. For instance, "I would
prefer it if you focus first on your studies. But
I also believe that forcing you to avoid the
person you like won't do any good. So, let's
enter into an agreement. This way, we will both
determine our limitations and boundaries."

➲ **Select your words cautiously.** It is crucial to
express your words at a level that your child can
understand.

➲ **Learn to read your child's signals.** Watch
out for subtle signs that convey that they are
tired, busy, sick, or not ready for a big talk.

When it comes to topics about sex, the general rule
is to be truthful but still discreet. Our children live in
an extremely sexualized society. They have become

exposed to sexual language, behaviors, and images even before they're ready to handle them.

The following are some helpful tips on how you can talk about sex with your teen:

- ⟳ **Never downplay or discredit your child's feelings.** Sure, you might have a different description and opinion about love from that of your child's. But their perspective and definition of love are equally important as yours. They deserve the respect you could give about their feelings and emotions.

- ⟳ **Do not overuse the "don'ts."** Traditional parents tend to impose strict rules laden with a series of *thou shall not*—"Don't go into a relationship," "Don't have sex," or "Don't get (someone) pregnant." Despite this straightforward approach, teenagers tend to rebel and disobey more, generating quite the opposite of the parents' desired results.

Instead of don'ts, why not use the dos? What can they do while in a relationship? What should they do to be sexually healthy with their girlfriend or boyfriend? What can they do to deal with a partner who pressures them to do sex? How can they determine whether a person is a potential romantic partner or a sexual partner? Discuss various options with them instead of trying to control their life with overwhelming rules.

➲ **Dispel myths, rumors, half-truths, and misinformation.** Your child has the right to know the truth, not fallacies. Just because you want a convenient way to stop them from doing what you think is wrong, you don't want to instill fear in their young minds. One example is telling your child that having sex makes them a pervert who deserves the fires of hell.

Give them accurate information. Explain facts in simple language but exercise respect in their curiosity and level of intelligence. When your twelve-year-old child asks what sex is all about, find out why they ask about it and give an honest answer that satisfies their curiosity.

➲ **Empower your teenager.** Teach them about their rights even as they enter a relationship.

For example, tell them that they deserve to be respected, keep their existing friendship, have their own space and privacy, and feel good about themselves.

Let them know that safety is non-negotiable. One of your parental priorities is to keep your child safe from threats, harm, or disease. Emphasize that nothing matters more than their safety. Tell this to them clearly and regularly. It would help to create a code word that serves as an SOS message whenever they feel that a situation turns out to be potentially dangerous or threatening. Teach them how to be safe from unwanted pregnancy or sexually transmitted diseases regardless of whether you agree with their decision to be in a sexual relationship or not. Always tell them that they can come to you for help whenever they feel troubled or abused.

➲ **Understand that teaching your child about sex doesn't mean you're disregarding family values.** Acknowledging sexuality does not equate to condoning or allowing your children to have sex whenever and wherever. It simply means that you want to help your children understand that having sexual thoughts and feelings is normal. It also allows you to explain further how they can manage urges or impulses or how abstinence can be beneficial for them. It gives enough opportunity for conversation and further learning how to be safe and responsible.

Ↄ **Speak in generalities.** Keeping it generic enables you to talk about controversial topics without getting uncomfortable. For instance, set other people and their experiences as examples to avoid making the case too personal. Also, avoid asking your child the specifics of what happened on their date or what they already did sexually.

Ↄ **Build a toolkit about sexuality.** Create your dossier of resources that aligns with your family values. They could be information from the internet or books. Just make sure that these came from credible sources and provide reliable information and advice. You can also look for other resources in your community, such as clinics, support groups, hotlines, or specialists.

UNDERSTANDING TEENAGE SEXUALITY

Sexuality is an essential part of who your child is and who they will become in the future. It changes and develops over time; thus, it is vital for your child to feel comfortable with their sexuality and sexual identity.

Sexuality doesn't automatically mean sex. It is about how your teenager:

- ➲ Feels about their changing and developing body.
- ➲ Renders sound decisions and choices about their own body.
- ➲ Understands and expresses feelings of attraction, affection, and intimacy for other people.
- ➲ Creates and maintains healthy, respectful relationships.

Remember, your child's expectations and beliefs about sexuality and sex are based on their personal experiences, cultural background, religion, and upbringing.

Parents will always be their child's first role model. You can teach your child by modeling and reinforcing values about responsibility, honesty, safety, and respect in relationships by treating your partner with love and respect.

Many teenagers experiment with sexual behavior at some point, something which is entirely natural and normal. During teen years, young people are maturing emotionally and socially. They often find themselves having sexual thoughts and attraction. They desire romantic intimacy and express their love and affection. Some may even want to explore adult behavior.

Some teenagers get sexually attracted to people of the opposite sex, while others tend to be attracted to the same sex. Some get sexually attracted to both, people of the same sex and opposite sex, and others have no sexual interest at all.

For some, these feelings can be confusing and intense, especially for those who experience attraction to someone belonging to a similar sex. They will begin to question their sexuality, and for those in a conservative family, it can be genuinely stressful.

You should understand that sexual identity and sexual attraction are two different things. One cannot simply say that a young person attracted to another person of the same sex is automatically lesbian, gay, or bisexual. They might be considered heterosexual or pansexual. It's only normal for young people to be attracted and have sexual thoughts about others of the same sex and the opposite sex. It's one of the processes they go through to sort out emerging sexual feelings.

Sexual attraction differs from gender identity as well. Gender identity pertains to a person's sense of who they are— a female, male, both, or neither. It may or may not also be shown in a person's sexual orientation and preferences in their sexual or romantic partner.

Your child's sexuality might differ from yours and your own expectations. However, it would be best for your child's interest if you could accept their sexuality. Your acceptance will help considerably in the development of their well-being and your relationship with them.

ENCOURAGING OPEN COMMUNICATION ABOUT SEXUALITY

Whether you accept it or not, your child will learn a lot about sexuality at school, with their friends, and online. Before they could get the corrupted version about this subject, you might as well have a heart-to-heart talk with them about sex and sexuality.

Talking about sex and sexuality with your child will help them classify information about sexuality from other sources. It will also persuade your child to create positive and sound choices in the present as well as in the future.

Of course, these conversations will be uncomfortable at first, but you can help mitigate it through the following:

Use the media for daily opportunities to talk about sexuality and relationships no matter how good, bad, or ugly they may be. Use topics introduced in popular teen culture as an impetus for theoretical conversations about sex and teen relationships. As much as possible, avoid imposing judgment and condemnation, even about fictional characters. Your child will mentally note your negative reactions and believe these as bases of your future response should they get to the same situation.

⮑ Let your child know that you are interested in their opinions and perspective. For instance, ask them what they think about sexuality or gender identity.

⮑ Ask your child what they already know or understand about a specific topic. Find out what they think about friendship, relationships, or sexual experiences. Ask questions such as, "What do you think about being in a romantic relationship at age 15?" or "How do you feel about your friends having a boyfriend or girlfriend?" Instead of throwing them questions answerable with yes or no, opt for open-ended questions. Understand, and do not judge your child. It is beneficial to talk about their friends and social circles. Teens generally like to talk about their friends and the people they socialize with more than they do about themselves. However, listening to their stories about their friends will provide you enough information and insight into how your teen feels and behaves.

➲ Be ready to talk about various concerns and issues when your child puts them forward. Assure them that you don't feel embarrassed having them ask those questions. On the other hand, be honest when you don't know how to answer their question. You could suggest that both of you look for the answer together instead.

COPING WITH BREAKUPS AND HEARTACHES IN TEENAGE RELATIONSHIPS

As adults, we all know too well that there is a possibility of dealing with breakups and heartaches when we enter into a relationship. Although our kids might also understand this, breakups are still especially hard for young hearts. Making matters worse is social media, which can play a part in worsening this real-life drama.

As parents, it's heartbreaking for us to see our children in pain and suffering. Nevertheless, we must also understand that this experience will mold them into the beautiful adult they should be. Breakups and heartaches are learning processes that they have to learn to manage difficult decisions, frustrations, and disappointments; after all, these are all part of life. That even though there is pain, they can discover the beauty of loving and living.

You must understand that your child might need time and space during this time, a confidant who is willing to listen or lend a shoulder to cry on. They may also need someone who will help them get distracted. Try not to force them out of their distress before they are emotionally ready.

Active listening will help you determine your child's needs. However, if your child seems depressed for more than a couple of weeks, you might need to get some advice or help from a health professional.

WHAT IF YOUR TEEN WAS SEXUALLY ASSAULTED OR ABUSED?

It is indeed devastating for your child to be sexually assaulted or abused. It can be a traumatizing event but also a life-changing one for your teen. It is one of those times when they need you most to support them.

To show you support and compassion, you have to listen and let them know that you aren't alone. It's good when your teens choose to tell you what happened to them and not just keep it to themselves – afraid that they'll be judged and blamed. Even if you think they are partly to blame, you have to constantly remind yourself that the sole blame is on the person who committed the crime. Your child is only a victim here and must not feel that you will blame them for what happened.

Help your child get the assistance they need – from health or medical care up to legal aid. If the assault or abuse just happened, they need immediate medical attention.

As your child needs to undergo therapy or join some community group, you can always show your support by being on their side at all times.

Never force your teen to do something that is not their will. Don't force them if they decide to keep silent on the issue and do not want to take legal action. However, if they choose to report to proper authorities, help them through every step.

HOW TO HELP YOUR TEEN WHO IS IN AN ABUSIVE RELATIONSHIP?

As a parent, we always want the best for our kids, which is why parents are too strict with their teen's relationship. We do not wish to have our child end up in an abusive relationship, but we can never tell what will happen. Being in a toxic and offensive relationship can always result in severe consequences like trauma, physical injury, and sometimes, death. Regardless of gender, your teen child can become a victim of abuse in an unhealthy relationship.

You may have done your part in teaching your teen how to spot signs of an abusive relationship, but the rest is up to them. If they choose to fall entrapped in a toxic relationship, it is because they allow it to happen to them.

When this happens, the best thing you can do is to let your teen know that you are always there for them no matter what happens and that you want them safe because you love them.

In an abusive relationship, the one to blame is the one committing and not the victim, so never make your teen feel that they are blamed for what happened.

172

Instead, make them think that they can openly talk to you about anything. In showing your support, focus on the action or what the abusive partner has done instead of blaming.

Try to encourage your son or daughter to cut the toxic relationship as soon as possible and that they are always welcome to come back home and won't be big trouble to you. Sometimes, it takes a long time before a final breakup.

YOUR TEEN AND UNWANTED PREGNANCY

While we want to keep our teens away from relationship issues like unwanted pregnancy, we can't deny that many of today's young people are getting pregnant at a very young age. Here are some conversation tips to help you prevent your child from getting into such a situation.

It will be much easier to talk to your teen about relationship issues if you have these questions in mind.

- ➲ What are your views on sexually active young people?
- ➲ Are they prepared to become parents?

➲ Should parents encourage their teens to use contraceptives?

➲ Were you sexually active while in your teens? How do you feel about it now as a parent?

It is important to talk with your children early and often about sex, love, and relationship. Knowing and finding out what your teen already understands by listening actively and maintaining an open conversation - making it a two-way conversation.

Discussing sex with your kids would not encourage them to be sexually active but help them understand how relationships work.

Talking openly with your kids makes them aware of your values and beliefs, so make sure that you do what you say to be a good role model.

When your teen feels comfortable asking you anything about relationships, you can rest assured that you will be the first person they will run to for help and support when they face some relationship challenges later. So make sure to let your kids know that they can talk to you about anything that worries them.

Here are some of the many things that teens want to discuss and know about.

- ⮆ How to identify true love from attraction?
- ⮆ Will sex bring you together closer?
- ⮆ How to tell my partner that I don't consider premarital sex without hurting them?
- ⮆ How to respond appropriately when my partner pressures me to have sex?
- ⮆ Do contraceptives work?
- ⮆ Can you get pregnant the first time you have sex?

Dealing with these questions is not easy, especially when they come from your kid. However, **be clear when bringing your points across and ensure that these are taken by your teens**, like:

- ⮆ I firmly believe that sex is an expression of love within the bounds of marriage and not outside of it.
- ⮆ Teenagers, especially in high school, are too young to have sex, especially with the danger and risks of AIDS and other sexually transmitted diseases.

➲ It is natural to have sexual desires or think about sex, but doing sex when you're not ready for pregnancy is incorrect or appropriate.

➲ Sex is not the only way to show your love to your partner.

➲ Having a baby does not transform a boy into a man or a girl into a woman. It means more responsibility for a new life that you bring into this world. So it would be best if you waited that you are ready for the responsibilities of parenthood before having a child.

➲ Sex does not enforce a healthy relationship. It does the opposite. If you have to pay the price for having a close relationship with sex, look for another partner who does not require it.

There is more to this long list of things you can do to prevent your daughter from unwanted pregnancy.

Again, we can see how important communication is in establishing a healthy and strong relationship with your teens. When peer pressures abound, your strong connection with your teens serves as their lifeline to reality while facing all these struggles in life. Therefore, make sure that the bond that connects you to your child is light enough for them to carry but strong enough to pull them back when they fell off the track.

Chapter 8

BECOMING MONEY SMART

*W*hether you like it or not, in a few years, your children will be on their own and make their way through the world armed with whatever lessons they learned from you. To prepare for their life ahead, equipping them with financial literacy is one of the most significant advantages you can give them.

If your teen can manage their finances, they can live independently from you without worrying too much about them. They will definitely enjoy a higher standard of living and have a greater sense of financial independence.

TIPS FOR GETTING CONVERSATION STARTED

Many parents often focus on many things other than talking to their child about money matters.

However, learning to manage finances even at a young age is a critical skill that your teenage child must learn. Help them get ready for their future by teaching them self-reliance and independence. You can start this by teaching them how to be financially responsible.

Teach Your Teens the Value of Savings

When discussing money matters with your teens, focus on values that affect your decision-making. Make them understand early why building a savings account is essential and how it can help them get out of trouble, especially during an economic crisis.

In teaching them about budgeting, emphasize that they should not spend more than they earn, and as much as possible avoid having debts. Without debts, you can live with less worry and enjoy the money you are making.

Promote Financial Awareness in the Family

Once your child reaches teenage years, they are old enough to understand money matters, and the earlier you expose them to financial issues at home, the easier it is for them to gain financial literacy. Allow them to join in family meetings about budgeting and spending. Although parents have the final say as the significant decision-makers, letting your teens understand your family's financial goal will encourage them to do their part, especially in saving. For example, everyone in the family needs to tighten their belt when saving for a college education. Once you have reached a particular milestone, they can also join in celebrating.

Let Them Participate in Decision-Making

When you are discussing budgeting and savings with your teen, consider using some visual aids. For example, show them your monthly bill and explain where the cost came from. If they know how much money is spent on electricity, they may suggest how to cut on those expenses, like turning off the lights, TV, computer, gadgets, or appliances while not in use.

Implement necessary cost-cutting measures involving the whole family. After a month, review the new monthly bills and see the effects of their choices to cut expenses.

In a way, you can challenge your children on how much the family could save and set a reward like a bit of celebration at home.

Provide Them the Opportunity to Earn

One way to teach your kids financial literacy is to encourage them to make their own money.

Whether it is in the form of taking an after-school or summer job or selling something in their spare time, exposing kids to these opportunities will go a long way.

For example, when your kid wants a new cellphone, instead of buying them a new one, tell them to save a portion of their allowance so they can buy it. The earlier your teen learns how to handle and give value to their savings or earnings, the better financial managers they will become later in life.

Discussing with your teens how their savings and spending habits will affect their future will create awareness of how current life choices determine their future. Also, don't forget to teach them about giving and sharing with others, for the more you give, the more you will receive.

THINGS TEENS WASTE MONEY ON

Fashion and music trends may have changed much compared to what it was three decades ago. However, like before, teens nowadays spend or waste their money on whatever seems to be worth their money at the moment, be it a blockbuster movie, a new video game, or concert tickets for a particular music artist they've been following right now.

182

According to statistics, Gen Z teens spend around two thousand dollars every year. Even though it's perfectly okay for them to spend their own money as they like, teens should know better than to spend every dime on random stuff.

Listed below are some of the things teenagers nowadays spend or waste their money on:

Fast Food and Beverages

Teens are constantly eating, probably because of the hormonal effects during their puberty stages. The truth is, food is the first thing teenagers spend their money on. They won't even hesitate to spend around fifteen dollars for a spicy chicken sandwich or whatever suits their palate at the moment.

Online Shopping

Before the pandemic, teens usually spend time browsing online shopping sites and buying things that piqued their interest. It might be all right to buy stuff online since it's generally cheaper and you do not have to go outside. The downside to this, however, is that kids do not feel the pain of using and losing cash, which results in reckless and impulsive spending.

Gadgets

Because gadgets are more advanced compared to the trending ones before, no teenager will just let the opportunity of having those slip from their hands. Nowadays, simply having the latest iPhone model can become a status symbol to those who have it. And since teenagers are naturally attention-seekers, they won't bat an eye even if they have to spend hundreds of dollars for it.

In-App Purchases

If you're using mobile phone apps like NETFLIX or play games like LEAGUE OF LEGENDS MOBILE, CALL OF DUTY MOBILE, and much more, you must be aware of the so-called "In-App Purchases." This term refers to any In-App service or perk that requires payment, which could be in the form of in-game currency, monthly subscriptions, and much more. If your teen happens to be a gamer, expect them to spend their money on games.

Trendy Shoes, Dress, and Cosmetics

Teenagers also take pride in their style, including stuff that is a part of the latest fashion trend like clothes, shoes, cosmetics, and bags advertised on television and the internet. And just like gadgets, those things are also a status symbol for those who have them.

Video Games and Consoles

The primary form of home entertainment for kids way back three decades ago were video games and game consoles which continue to come out almost every year. It is not surprising anymore if there is a new version of the game console or the latest installment of the game you've been a fan of is released. In such a case, teens and adults alike (who are long-time fans) will not hesitate to pay hundreds of dollars to get that firsthand.

Concert Tickets

Teens naturally identify themselves with music, so it's not unusual for them to watch a concert or two of their favorite artists or band whenever they can. And the closer their seat is to the stage, the more expensive their tickets are.

School Dances or Parties

Participating in school events can be expensive, especially if you have to follow a particular dress code like in proms. Buying or renting clothes, getting a car, and going out to dinner can hurt not only the teen's wallet but also their parent's.

Dates

Regardless of their gender, teens going on a date require them to spend money. So the more expensive their dates are, the faster their money flies.

Spring Break or Vacation Trips

Outgoing teens tend to spend some of their vacation time with their friends. Such trips usually involve going somewhere away from their home city where they can relax. However, doing such things is possible as long as you have enough money to spend on it.

FINANCIAL LITERACY FOR TEENS

After a few years, long-time parents should know that talking to their teenage children about anything can be pretty challenging. However, it does not mean that they should skip on it, especially when it comes to teaching financial management. And once they reach legal age, they will likely graduate, have their job, and finally move out of your house. It is reported that about seventy percent of college graduates in the US learned the skills straight from their parents. However, no one knows how those parents opened this tricky topic to them.

MONEY MANAGEMENT AND TEENS

Just like those talks about adolescence and puberty-related issues you're bound to relay this information to your teens, so financial discussions should be open and honest. It may be somewhat sensitive, just like whenever parents talk to their kids about sex and drugs but more challenging to explain. However, speaking to teens about finances requires a considerably longer time than the other two topics, so teaching them earlier is necessary. Start teaching them about budgeting, needs, and savings early.

Budgeting Allowances

More than half of Generation Z says that they do not know how much they should spend and save from their money. In other words, they don't have a clue about budgeting. In such cases, giving them insights into the family budget will do the trick. It helps teens grasp the concept of savings, compound interest, delayed gratification, and expenses. Additionally, having the idea of budgeting helps teens handle their own money as efficiently as possible.

Start teaching your teen to allocate their funds into four different categories, namely: Expenses, Savings, Investments, and Charity. You can also teach teens about the 50/30/20 rule of budgeting, wherein the 50% goes to essential expenses, 30% goes to personal spending, and the remaining 20% goes to savings. For teens, having a clear concept of where their money should go is easy to follow and can be perfected through lots of practice.

Credit Cards

It is a well-known fact that giving your child a credit card can be a scary thing. However, it is necessary despite being troublesome. After all, helping teens learn the concept of credit and credit history is also a significant financial lesson. Parents can teach their teens about this by starting with a teen-friendly credit card having a low spending limit. You can also use a secured credit card that requires a security deposit that serves as its credit limit.

Listed below are some of the credits cards available to teens in the US:

Discover It Secured Credit Card

This is considered one of the best credit card choices for building credit. It requires clients to put up a security deposit before teens can use them. You can also choose the deposit amount up to its approved credit limit. Additionally, this card builds credit history with the three major credit card bureaus (Equifax, Experian, and TransUnion) and has bonuses and no fees.

Journey Student Rewards from Capital One

Created just for students, this is an excellent option for starters since it has no annual fee. It is meant to build a positive credit history, and a $0 fraud liability covers its users. Users can also set up automatic payments and qualify for a higher credit line if they maintain a good credit history for six months.

Apple Card

Apple card is built straight into iPhones for teens aged 18 years and above, so it is there as long as the iPhone is not lost or destroyed. Apple Cards are easy to use, and the customer service is reachable via iMessage whenever you need them. It can also send out weekly and monthly credit reports so teens and parents alike can easily monitor their spending activities.

BEST BUDGET TOOLS AND WORKSHEETS FOR TEENS

Whenever teens start writing numbers up, they quickly get hit on the head with reality. After all, numbers do not lie, and no one will ignore the truth after seeing tons of expenses written on paper. So whenever teens start suffering through a money blunder, you can sit down with them and help them out by identifying where things go wrong.

Teens must learn to budget since it is a critical part of financial management. Kindly take note that the so-called "mind budgeting" will not work. Why? Teens do not have enough experience with those, while adults can get away with it since they have been practicing it for years, if not decades. Additionally, one becomes more successful at following a budget plan if they start writing it.

For teens, who are just starting out on a budgeting journey, these are the best budget worksheets that they can use:

Entrepreneur Toolbox App

If your teen is budgeting for a specific goal or purpose, this app is for them. It features ways to budget and set savings goals and track its progress. One can start a new savings goal by inputting the amount to get, the finances you have right now, and the date or deadline for your specific monetary purpose. Once done, it tracks your progress daily.

Toshl App

A budgeting app for teens and adults alike, Toshl App has a fun but straightforward interface. It can connect itself with your teen's financial accounts, allowing automatic updates to track one's financial situation. There is also a manual option for updating their financial statement if your teen does not have a bank account.

Plan it Prom App

If you want your teen to learn budgeting in the simplest way possible, make them use the Prom app. Parents who know budgeting basics can teach them how to budget for an event or even teach them to budget in general. Teens can use this app and get an event countdown, such as how many days are left for the prom night, graduation ball, etc.

Money Prodigy's Teen Budget Worksheet

By using this app, your teen can become familiar with financial terms such as Expenses, Income Sources, Budget Cycle, Money Calendar, and Savings and understand its meaning. At the end of each budgeting cycle, they can review the sheet and fill out every column to monitor their expenses and earnings to determine their budget plan.

Quick Monthly Expense Tracker

Teens will likely work with this app due to its colorful user interface and layout. It can be an excellent way for teens to become aware of their earnings, balance, and spending.

Paycheck Budgeting Worksheet

If your teen is earning on a weekly, bi-weekly, or monthly basis, introducing them to paycheck budgeting and monitoring could be helpful for them. In this app, each budget cycle is synchronized with their paycheck cycle, which will help them determine how much of their actual money is left until their next payday.

CONCLUSION

*I*f there's anything you want in life as a parent, it's nothing more than having a good relationship with your teens. Having a good relationship is built through the years of good communication channels. Ideally you would start making these communication channels while your child is still young. You don't have to wait for them to be old enough to understand every word you say.

It can really be tough parenting teens and engage them in conversations. It can be too frustrating for you if you really want to connect with your teen.

However, we can't deny the fact that day-to-day situations can often interfere with parent-child conversations.

Building a strong relationship with your teens begins as early as when they start going to school or even before that. Remember that their childhood years are their formative years. While you are there beside them showing them how much you care and constantly engage them in real conversation, they will grow up to have a closer relationship with you. Not even when they're passing through their teenage years could they neglect that close ties with you in favor of new friends.

A child who is nurtured in care, love, discipline, values, and the right attitude will never forget what they learned in school. It starts from the house rules and lessons learned from their parents.

Teenagers that grow in a good family will literally be strong enough to stand on the good side and not be easily swayed by toxic people. Every habit they formed was because of those things that were instilled in them during their childhood.

It is for such reason that this conversation guide was written to help parents not only harness their communication skills but for them to effectively raise their kids into respectable, productive, and successful adults in the future.

REFERENCES

Better Health Channel. (n.d.). Teenagers and
communication – Better Health Channel.
Retrieved August 8, 2021,
https://www.betterhealth.vic.gov.au/health/healt
hyliving/teenagers-and-communication

Cleveland Clinic. (n.d.). Adolescent Development.
Retrieved August 8, 2021,
https://my.clevelandclinic.org/health/articles/70
60-adolescent-development

familyeducation.com. (2017, August 2). Battles Are
Part of Raising Teenage Daughters. Retrieved
August 8, 2021,
https://www.familyeducation.com/life/mother-
daughter-relationships/battles-are-part-raising-
teenage-daughters

Kid's Health. (n.d.). Nine Steps to More Effective
Parenting (for Parents) – Nemours Kidshealth.
Retrieved August 8, 2021,

https://kidshealth.org/en/parents/nine-steps.html

Langslet, K. (2020, August 5), 3 Signs a Person with Toxic Qualities Is Manipulating You (and What to Do About It). Retrieved August 8, 2021, https://greatist.com/live/dealing-with-a-toxic-person

Mississippi Deptarment of Transporation. (n.d.). Facts and Statistics – MS Safety Education. Retrieved August 8, 2021, https://mdot.ms.gov/safetyeducation/parents/facts-and-stats/

Revised Guidelines Redefine Birth Years and Classifications for Gen X, Millennials, and Generation Z. (2019, December 6). Retrieved August 8, 2021, https://www.mentalfloss.com/article/609811/age-ranges-millennials-and-generation-z

Rivara F. (2016, September 14). Consequences of Bullying Behavior – Preventing Bullying Through Science, Policy, and Practice – NCBI Bookshelf. Retrieved August 8, 2021,

https://www.ncbi.nlm.nih.gov/books/NBK3904
14/

VeryWell Family, & Morin, LCSW, A. (2019).
Common Mental Health Issues in Teens.
https://www.verywellfamily.com/common-
mental-health-issues-in-teens-2611241

Wojciechowski, M. (2021, August 7). How
Friendships Can Reduce Stress. Retrieved August
8, 2021,
https://www.medpagetoday.com/nursing/nursin
g/77619